"The Lord is recovering
something on this earth
which is absolutely different from
Christianity and any religion."
–*Witness Lee*[1]

THE GOD-MEN

An Inquiry into Witness Lee & the Local Church

Neil T. Duddy
& the SCP

InterVarsity Press
Downers Grove, Illinois 60515

Second edition © *1981 by Inter-Varsity Christian Fellowship of the United States of America*

First edition © *1977 by Inter-Varsity Christian Fellowship of the United States of America, published under the title* The God-Men: Witness Lee and the Local Church *(Spiritual Counterfeits Project).*

InterVarsity Press is the book-publishing division of Inter-Varsity Christian Fellowship, a student movement active on campus at hundreds of universities, colleges and schools of nursing. For information about local and regional activities, write IVCF, 233 Langdon St., Madison, WI 53703.

Distributed in Canada through InterVarsity Press, 1875 Leslie St., Unit 10, Don Mills, Ontario M3B 2M5, Canada.

Unless otherwise indicated, all biblical references are taken from the New American Standard Bible.

ISBN 0-87784-833-5
Library of Congress Catalog Card Number: 79-2806

Printed in the United States of America

18	17	16	15	14	13	12	11	10	9	8	7	6	5	4	3	2	1
95	94	93	92	91	90	89	88	87	86	85	84	83	82	81			

Publisher's Note

This book was originally scheduled for publication in early 1980. Just prior to its release, Local Church officials contacted the publisher and supplied further information about its beliefs and practices. This material was carefully reviewed by both the author and the publisher, resulting in some modifications and thereby a delay in publication in the interest of accuracy and fairness.

We believe that *The God-Men* will make a positive contribution to the broader understanding of this religious movement.

Preface

Telegraph Avenue, Berkeley, California
Midafternoon on a summer's day, 1972

Sunlight splotched its way through the steamy front windows of the laundromat, randomly striking washing machines, dryers and customers moving from one task to another.

Reaching into a washer with a sweaty arm to extract his denim overalls, Brooks Alexander heard the sound of drums approaching and people cheering. "A parade," he thought, wondering what it was all about. Through the windows he soon saw a chanting, pounding cadence of human beings throbbing up Telegraph Avenue toward the university. "O Lord Jesus, O Lord Jesus. Jesus is Lord. O Lord Jesus." With the other laundromat patrons, Brooks hurried outside.

The parade was almost ten blocks long. Hundreds of young people wearing flour sacks brandished placards on which Bible verses were lettered. The women were neat, the men clean-shaven, their ranks orderly. The longhaired, bearded onlookers of Berkeley's countercultural element, baffled at first, soon expressed their contempt. With straightened backs and clicking heels they shouted back, *"Sieg Heil!"* at the passing marchers. As Brooks stood silently watching, he felt a kind of chill.

That night Brooks Alexander tried to explain to some non-Christian friends that it was not "basic Christianity" that had paraded up the avenue that afternoon. Rather, the marchers represented something like a "Gnostic-Eastern Holy-Rollerism," he said, one point on a broad spectrum of Christian and pseudo-Christian factions (see *Gnosticism* in Glossary). But his friends couldn't understand. Most of Berkeley didn't understand. What was going on?

The parade had been sponsored by congregations of "the Local Church" in northern and southern California in an effort to evangelize Berkeley. They had marched on a street that symbolized both the freedom and the degradation of hedonistic humanism in post-Christian America. Theirs was a voice crying, chanting, in the wilderness, but a voice that had failed to communicate. The Local Church members had neither understood nor related to the crowd their drums had summoned.

That parade was an example of attempts by Local Church members to influence secular and Christian communities. Their efforts were designed to attract attention. They did attract attention, but to a group of "religious fanatics," not to any recognizable "good news." During the early 1970s, such parades were staged in Berkeley, throughout the state of California and elsewhere.

Local Church history is one of stormy relations with Christian churches critical of its doctrinal posture, its internal social relationships and its conduct in society. This book attempts to document Local Church doctrine and conduct. Our analysis and critique is based on many published writings of the Local Church's founder, Witness Lee, and on personal reports collated by the authors regarding Local Church interactions with communities nationwide. The authors have personally contacted Local Church leaders and members for the purpose of collecting firsthand information. Additional information has come from correspondence with persons who have been members of the Local Church, who have had encounters with Local Church members or who have conducted interviews with Local Church participants.

We have earnestly sought a personal audience with Witness Lee in order that our understanding of his teachings and practices might once and for all be substantiated or corrected. Before the initial printing of *The God-Men* by the Spiritual Counterfeits Project (SCP), a certified letter requesting an appointment with Lee and with two Local Church representatives was sent to Lee's home. The receipt was returned to our office, bearing Mrs. Lee's signature, but with no reply. After a reasonable wait, we sent Lee a telegram, again urging him to respond to our invitation to dialogue. We received no response.

Since publication of *The God-Men,* Witness Lee has continued to refuse dialog with staff of the Spiritual Counterfeits Project. Researcher Neil Duddy went twice to Local Church headquarters in Anaheim, California, and spoke with Lee's two chief apologists. At the close of the second session—a discussion of the concerns set forth in this revision of *The God-Men*—Duddy was told that Lee, for reasons of principle, does not respond to criticisms or questions from outsiders. Local Church executive Ronald R. Kangas was not inclined even to tell Lee that an SCP researcher had visited their headquarters. Dialogue, even to clarify points about Local Church doctrine and conduct, was obviously not being encouraged. The disposition of the Local Church toward such interaction was epitomized by Kangas's response to a question about Lee's unusual, extensive use of allegory: "You're not spiritual. You don't understand." When Duddy tried to reach Witness Lee at home by telephone, Mrs. Lee referred him back to Kangas.

A third visit to the Local Church's Anaheim headquarters during a Sunday morning teaching session provided an opportunity for our SCP researcher to introduce himself to

Witness Lee. Dominating the conversation that followed, Lee expressed anger toward the Spiritual Counterfeits Project and defended his teachings. Yet he avoided any direct response to the researcher's questions.

Because the Spiritual Counterfeits Project continues to receive many inquiries from concerned Christians across the nation and around the world, this updated report on the Local Church is being published. The recorded words of Witness Lee bear testimony to what he believes and teaches. The Local Church continues to endorse his writings. His disciples continue to accept his teachings as authoritative.

The Local Church and Witness Lee were invited to read our revised manuscript and were given the prerogative of attaching a five-page response to appear as an Appendix. Lee expressed his refusal to accept our offer in a certified letter dated May 22, 1979.

One of our sources of information on Local Church practices was Max D. Rapoport, who served as Witness Lee's right-hand man for more than four years, ending in 1978. A forceful, dynamic personality, Rapoport provided leadership and counsel for the Local Church nationally and internationally. His responsibilities included directing leaders' training sessions, drafting church policy and managing the church's business affairs. Rapoport eventually became Lee's most intimate associate and favored confidant. Then, as president of the Anaheim Local Church and a member of the board of directors of Living Stream, Inc., Rapoport became convicted about Local Church practices and for eighteen months sought to instigate reform. He gradually slipped from his status as Lee's heir apparent and finally was publicly denounced before the Local Churches in Orange County. A videotape of that meeting was sent to all the other Local Churches in the U.S. By that time he had left the Local Church, accompanied by a number of other disquieted members. Lee and Local Church officials have decried Rapaport's

defection and labeled him a lost son of perdition. Rapoport
and his associates, however, have opted for biblical truth,
sound practice and open fellowship with all Christians.

In Rapoport's appraisal, "Lee's attempts to restate biblical teachings in nontraditional theological vocabulary
have almost inevitably led to misunderstanding." Many
times Lee speaks or writes to fit the need of the moment as
he seeks to control the so-called "flow" and direction of all
the Local Churches. Rapoport asserts, however, that Lee is
not a "modalist" (see Glossary). Nor, according to Rapoport,
does Lee believe that "mingling" deifies Christian converts,
even though Lee's oral teachings, writings and illustrations
appear to affirm both a modalistic Godhead and the deification of believers. Rapoport believes that Lee personally
holds a more biblical view than many of his words indicate.

Finally, the Spiritual Counterfeits Project has suggested
to Witness Lee's publisher, Ron Kangas, that a companion
guide to Lee's writings be published, to explain any confus-
ing or misleading statements. To date, neither the Local
Church nor its associated organization, Living Stream, Inc.,
has done so. Since Witness Lee has declined to discuss theological issues with us personally, we are left with his teachings, writings, illustrations and responses to earlier criticism of Local Church practices and beliefs as the only official
documentation to evaluate the Local Church movement.

Neil Duddy, Researcher
Brooks Alexander, Director
Spiritual Counterfeits Project
Berkeley, California
November 1980

1

The Local Church:
An Enquiry

Christian belief and conduct must always align themselves with the contours of biblical instruction. God's inspired Scripture provides criteria for measuring belief and conduct, and in orthodox Christian groups or communities right belief and right conduct are generated by the power of biblical teaching.

Our Biblical Guidelines
Evangelical Christians regard the Bible as the authoritative source for teaching on morality and social propriety, as well as theology. As the apostle Paul wrote to the elder-teacher Timothy, "All Scripture is inspired by God [God-breathed] and profitable for teaching, for reproof, for correction, for training in righteousness; that the man of God may be adequate, equipped for every good work" (2 Tim. 3:16-17).

Many of Paul's letters emphasize a need for *orthopraxis* in addition to orthodoxy, that is, for both "right doing" and "right teaching," guided by Scripture (see Glossary).

The first letter of John underscores that concern and embellishes Paul's instruction to Timothy to derive all the teachings for his own personal ministry from Scripture. In addition, John required all Christians to evaluate the ministry of their elder-teachers by using scriptural guidelines.

In his commentary *The Epistles of John,* John R. W. Stott notes the need for Christian communities to evaluate their teachers using Scripture as their base. Focusing on 1 John 2, Stott recommends the application of three tests, two of which are a social test and a doctrinal test.[1] These enable a Christian community to recognize the sometimes alluring falsities of *pseudopraxis* and heterodoxy among its teachers.

Stott points first to 1 John 2:9-10, one of many passages in that epistle emphasizing that Christian teachers are to exhibit moral and social behavior appropriate to God's children: "The one who says he is in the light and yet hates his brother is in the darkness until now. The one who loves his brother abides in the light and there is no cause for stumbling in him." An instructor whose relationships within the Christian community are consistently abrasive and fraught with strife has, by biblical definition, run askew.

Stott cites 1 John 2:24-25 as one of many texts demanding doctrinal purity from Christian teachers: "let that abide in you which you heard from the beginning. If what you heard from the beginning abides in you, you also will abide in the Son and in the Father." As Stott points out, the apostle John required Christians to measure the teachings of their instructors by the apostolic teachings.[2] Right doctrine is related to remaining "in the Son and in the Father." Conversely, false doctrine leads to the breaking of that bond.

The Local Church has presented itself as the harbinger of revived Christianity, the vanguard and supreme instructor of the church. For the reasons drawn from Scripture by John Stott, we are obliged to evaluate both the *teachings* of the Local Church and its *interactions* with surrounding Christian communities. The apostle John's model for such evaluation provides the rationale, framework and guidelines for this study.

Contagious Zeal

Exuberant joy is contagious, especially when focused on God, his Word and his church. Today we are faced by various religious movements that promote their teachings and lifestyles with great zeal, especially among young people. Such movements have strong appeal to those whose experience in and out of the church has been dull and unsatisfying. Here at last is lively commitment! Whatever their finer points of doctrine, at least the adherents are enthusiastic about their fellowship.

"Zeal for Thy house has consumed me"; Jesus Christ's dramatic cleansing of the temple in Jerusalem reminded his disciples of that line from Psalm 69:9. Christ's zeal for God's house laid a foundation for the Christian church.[3] It set a pattern of zeal for God's people to follow.

But the Bible also warns that zeal may be misplaced. Paul lamented over his Jewish kinsmen's plight: "they have a zeal for God, but it is not enlightened." He foresaw a time when some even in the Christian community would be "holding the form of religion but denying the power of it." His counsel was to avoid such people.[4]

The followers of Witness Lee both stress and exemplify the way of commitment and zeal in church life. They see themselves as "the Lord's overcomers," the "recovered church" of the last days. They are understandably excited about what they believe to be their unique participation in God's plan. For Christians outside their movement, however, the Local Church raises many questions that are difficult to answer satisfactorily.

By examining the Local Church movement closely, we hope to achieve an understanding of its teachings and practices. Thus we hope to discern whether those who follow Witness Lee's direction are zealous in ways that please the Lord and deserve our emulation, or whether their enthusiasm masks a departure from an authentic understanding of God. Some four years of research and experience lie behind this undertaking.

Getting the Facts

Witness Lee is a tireless speaker and writer. Despite his prolific output, little effort has been made within the Local Church to arrange the movement's theological distinctives in a way that can easily be grasped. Consequently, a major part of our effort has been devoted to drafting what is, in effect, an outline for a "systematic theology of the Local Church." We have tried to structure the doctrine (that is, teaching) of Witness Lee so that it can be apprehended as a whole, rather than in fragments. That purpose has influenced the organization of our material.

The main body of this book is devoted to an exposition of what we understand to be the position of Lee and his movement on a number of traditional theological categories, along with our response to those positions. The areas of theology discussed are those considered essential to the structure of any well-balanced biblical theology. They are not picayune topics revolving around secondary or tertiary truths. Although distilling the fundamental tenets of Lee's theology from his voluminous writings is not easy, we believe we have portrayed his theology fairly and accurately.

A particular problem of trying to summarize Local Church teaching is worth noting in anticipation of whatever response Witness Lee or his spokespersons may wish to make to this revision of *The God-Men*. The psychological dynamic or spiritual experience taught by the Local Church is described as a subjective experience giving a "standard of spirituality" that is "extremely vague and obscure."[5] The experience of God is viewed as noncommunicable; it is non-cognitive, nonpropositional. It is sensed, felt, even smelled or tasted. Yet at the same time, that subjective spiritual experience, though lacking an objective measure for growth and maturity in Christ, is regarded as a fundamental and absolute requirement for experiencing the true "Reality."

When the "vague and obscure" are absolutized, precision, their opposite, is deprecated almost as a matter of course. For example, any attempts to approach biblical language as a vehicle of meaning in the ordinary sense, or to use one's rational faculties to grasp that meaning, are routinely relegated by the Local Church to a status so inferior as to be virtual evidence of a "backslidden" condition. The stress is always on subjective experience.

Under such circumstances, it is not surprising that the conceptual structure and logical consistency of Local Church doctrine are somewhat loose. In all of Witness Lee's writings there is not a single major statement that is not elsewhere qualified in several different directions. Sometimes major statements are turned on their heads altogether by the affirmation of contradictory points. Such confusion occurs in Lee's teaching on the doctrine of God, Christology, the inspiration of Scripture, the role of the law in ethics and discerning the will of God.

Do They or Don't They?

It appears, further, that Witness Lee has hammered out a double-edged sword, one blade symbolizing biblical literalism and the other extrabiblical teaching. The latter, although sheathed in biblical terminology, constitutes an unusual shading or, possibly, a twisting of Scripture.

The ramifications of that situation are twofold. First, by

using biblical terminology, the Local Church gains easy access into Christian communities where the Bible is revered. Second, when criticized or accused of unbiblical teaching, the Local Church is able to produce true biblical affirmations. Certainly the presence of biblical teaching in their ministry must be acknowledged. Yet major emphasis is placed on unusual, obscure or questionable points of doctrine. That emphasis generates friction between Local Church assemblies and the larger Christian community.

The Local Church mentality evidently has no difficulty in accommodating contradiction in a variety of forms. It is not uncommon to find Local Church leaders behaving in ways that exemplify the errors they decry in others (that is, in "Christianity"). For example, Witness Lee says that "doctrine only works divisions among the Lord's children" and "the more we talk about doctrines, the more we will quarrel."[6] At the same time, he not only teaches but insists upon certain doctrines (such as "mingling" and "local ground") in a way that leads him to reject fellowship with every major Christian body in the world.

Another example of contradiction between word and action is found in Local Church techniques of proselyting. While professing a concept of doctrineless unity, a unity based on spiritual experience and submission, the Local Church carries out a program of church growth that seems to be based on almost arbitrary divisiveness.

Securing converts among people seeking "a New Testament-type church," the Local Church took people away from a number of already-established groups. The pattern was almost always the same.

Contact was made with a group that had some ideas similar to those of the Local Church. There would be a great deal of talk about unity. Slowly the group would lean towards some kind of co-working with the Local Church.

As soon as the Local Church was in a position to take a sizeable portion of the other group, some issue would be made. It didn't make any difference what issue. Just an issue. A stand with one side or the other was then demanded by the Local Church. They, of course, could no longer work together with a false church that had now shown its real colors. The ugly head of sectarianism had risen. No way would the Local Church accept that. Division resulted, and the Local Church took its spoils of victory away.[7]

Considering Lee's radical deprecation of doctrine and his downgrading of any intellectual appraisal of doctrinal orthodoxy, it is worth asking why the Local Church exercises itself so strenuously to present an appearance of holding to orthodox beliefs. For example, why did the Local Church spend $40,000 in newspaper advertisements to refute *The God-Men* when it was first published by the Spiritual Counterfeits Project, while claiming orthodoxy in the same breath? In those ads, the Local Church outlined the necessary and fundamental articles of orthodox Christian faith, quoted historical figures considered important in biblical Christianity and then referred to several persons associated with "deeper life" teaching as holding views similar to theirs.

One Local Church publication, *A Reply to the Tract against Witness Lee and the Local Church,* contains a ten-point credo in substantially orthodox language. Yet it makes no explicit mention of the Local Church's controversial doctrines or their low opinion of "Christianity."[8] Likewise the Local Church has placed newspaper advertisements making the same claims. Our experience and that of others convinces us that they present such semblances of orthodoxy and don the mantle of evangelical authenticity primarily for strategic purposes. They hope to recruit Christians into their movement after disarming their critical scrutiny.

Putting It All Together

The present study contains two major sections: theological and sociological. The sociological follows the theological assessment because the practical, logical extensions of Witness Lee's thought are directly responsible for Local Church members' methods of interacting with Christian and secular communities. Readers who want only a phenomenological view of the Local Church, or who find theology somewhat dry, may wish to read the latter section as an independent study.

In our treatment of the theological content of Witness Lee's teaching, we have attempted to restrict most of our critique to a separate chapter evaluating Lee's thought as a whole. Total separation of exposition and evaluation has not been possible, but where our appraisals occur, they should be evident. Our quotations from Lee's writings are intended as illustrations of his beliefs rather than as "proof texts" for any of his theological positions.

Several things that we have *not* attempted to do in this study should be noted:

1. We have not tried to answer such questions as "Is Witness Lee a Christian?" or "Are members of the Local Church saved?" Whatever one's personal opinions on such matters, both questions are biblically inappropriate for our present purposes. Christian men and women, even if sometimes misguided or ill-informed, do belong to Local Church congregations. The nucleus of this book is rather an attempt to answer the question: "Does the doctrine of Witness Lee and the Local Church present a picture of God, Christ, the human condition and Christian responsibilities in a needy world that is true to the content of biblical revelation?" That is an answerable question which Scripture constrains us to address.[9]

2. We have not tried to produce an exhaustive catalog of Local Church teaching. Rather, our effort has been to cap-

ture the thrust of Witness Lee's approach to certain major themes.

3. We have not tried to make a scientific study of the Local Church's social dynamics. Our national and international correspondents describe the character of Local Church relationships only within their respective communities. We have found, however, a high degree of uniformity in their observations and experiences.

Nonetheless, as we begin our examination, we are well aware of Witness Lee's viewpoint on such an undertaking: "In my entire Christian life I have never seen one Christian who, when he criticized and opposed the local churches, was ever blessed by the Lord from that time forth. I have observed that all those who have opposed the church life have become backsliders. There has not been one exception. Let them all be put to shame and turned backward. It is not a small thing. . . . If you hate the local churches, you will have no more growth of life. There will be no rich reaping and no rich harvest."[10] Such a statement in effect amounts to a curse on critics of Lee's teachings. It portends evil to any members of Local Church fellowships with qualms about their personal involvement. It is equivalent to a pronouncement that God himself will blight those who oppose the Local Church. It parallels the "woes" listed in Old Testament prophetic writings exhorting the Israelites to obedience. And it dovetails with Lee's view that the Local Church is the only true church.

We take no delight in publishing this assessment. We would be glad if we could answer our inquirers with assurance that Witness Lee's teachings do not differ from the teaching of God's Word. But we are convinced otherwise and we believe that the dangers of his system should be made known.

As researchers, we write out of concern for the high standard of God's truth to which all who profess his name are

called and held. Our goal is not controversy, self-vindica-
tion or financial profit. Rather, we are concerned to protect
the broad Christian community and to call Witness Lee and
the Local Church to accountability, that God's people might
be truly free as God has promised.[11]

2

History of the Movement:
A Short Overview

Witness Lee was born in China around the turn of the century and was influenced by the reaction of some Chinese churches against Western missionary practices. Christianity has always been identified in the minds of many Chinese people with Western imperialism.

Watchman Nee and the Little Flock in Asia
One dissatisfied Chinese Christian was Watchman Nee (1903-72), probably the single strongest influence on Lee's ideas and leadership role. Nee's disenchantment with the sterile formalism of his Christian education led him to help start a "house church" of the Plymouth Brethren type in Foochow in 1922. At the same time, Nee was introduced to certain writings on the spiritual life, including those of Madame Guyon, Jessie Penn-Lewis, Andrew Murray and

J. N. Darby. Those writers spoke of an inner, spiritual, somewhat mystical life and union with Christ, and of an informal, autonomous church structure with almost no distinction between clergy and laity.

In the late 1920s, Watchman Nee completed a book, *The Spiritual Man,* in which he taught that human nature is composed of three parts: body, soul and spirit. In Nee's view, the only acceptable qualities or activities were those that proceeded from the human spirit, the dormant part of an individual which comes alive through the activity of the Holy Spirit. Only the human *spirit* is indwelt by the Holy Spirit, which urges and produces intuitions in it that are then interpreted by the *soul* (that is, the mind). The human spirit divided from the soul and overpowering the soul is an influential teaching of Watchman Nee adopted by Witness Lee.

Nee moved to Shanghai and founded the first of his own churches, which came to be known as "the Little Flock." The new church was completely independent of all other churches in Shanghai. Ten years later, in 1938, Nee published *Concerning Our Missions* (later retitled *The Normal Christian Church Life),* spelling out the position he had begun to take in 1928:

1. Denominationalism is a sin and a detriment to spiritual growth. The church ought to be unified.

2. There is to be only one church within each geographic area, and that local church is to be independent of all other churches.

3. All believers ought to break away totally from the denominations and establish proper local churches.[1]

Witness Lee came into the Little Flock movement when it was beginning to flourish in the 1930s. As a child Lee had been taught Bible stories and such doctrines as dispensations[2] and the existence of two natures within redeemed people. Although he attended a Christian school, he was not converted until early adulthood. As a Christian he went through several changes. In 1927 he was elected a member of the executive committee of his denomination, but he refused the position and left the denomination. Five years later, in his words, he first "came into the local church." That same year he began ministering at the Little Flock of Chefoo in North China.

By the 1930s Witness Lee's cultural background, his personality and perhaps his Christian experience had produced in him an intense introspection. He was affected deeply by two kinds of alienation ultimately traceable to the human Fall: alienation from fellow human beings and alienation from one's self. Lee became extraordinarily careful not to offend anyone. He would not read a newspaper in another person's presence unless given permission; he would write a letter three or four times to be sure it was perfect; he would apologize for some minor offense several times in spite of being forgiven at the time of his initial apology. (Today Lee says we all must sometimes deal that severely with our consciences.)[3] The soil from which his own special "theology of experience" later sprang was thus being cultivated.

By the 1940s Witness Lee had become a close and invaluable associate of Watchman Nee. Lee had a flair for organization which Nee lacked. From 1939 to 1942 Nee helped Lee through informal training in Shanghai.[4]

Although Witness Lee was imprisoned by the Japanese military police in 1943 and had tuberculosis for three years after his release, he was back in Shanghai teaching from 1946 to 1948.[5] At a Little Flock workers' meeting in 1948, worker control over the local churches was established—a change in policy for Nee which evidently suited Lee, the organizer. "It appears that 1948 marked a turning point in Mr. Nee's church practices and the beginning of an hierarchical system of central control which differed little from the organization of denominational churches. There are, those who believe that here we are witnessing the growing influence of Witness Lee, who later was to exercise such autocratic control over the churches in Taiwan."[6] As the Communists were advancing on the mainland, Nee appointed Witness Lee as leader of the Little Flock of Taiwan.[7]

A dozen years later, serious splits developed in Taiwan and Hong Kong. Some in the churches of the Little Flock accepted Witness Lee's leadership. Others believed he had deviated from the teachings of Watchman Nee by introducing questionable doctrines and unscriptural forms of worship. A number of Little Flock leaders and assemblies in different cities of Southeast Asia cut their ties with Witness Lee. In spite of such internal conflicts within its established ranks, the Local Church has forged ahead with new outreach programs in the Philippines, Indonesia, Korea, Malaysia, and even in New Zealand, Germany, Switzerland, Brazil, Nigeria and the United States. The constituency of the Local Church outside of the United States is approximately 35,000 members.[8] In the United States and Canada, Local Church membership is estimated to be less than 7,000. Witness Lee's disciples number more than the Local Church membership, however. His widely read writings continue to influence people in spin-off groups both from the Local Church and from other Christian communities.

Witness Lee and the Local Church in America
Evidently, Witness Lee considered Taiwan his base until 1962, when he came to the United States and settled in the Los Angeles area.[9] Since then, southern California has been a stronghold of what is now known as the Local Church. In the late 1960s Lee began to use the "Jerusalem Principle" (derived from Acts 8:4) in the United States. That is, whole groups of Christians would emigrate to establish a church. A group of about seventy emigrated from California to Houston in 1969; others went to Seattle, Chicago, Akron and

Atlanta in 1970. By 1974 there were some forty or fifty Local Churches in the U.S.; in 1979, approximately fifty to sixty were in existence.

Local Church assemblies in the United States frequently do not identify themselves as adherents of Witness Lee's teachings. Rather, they present themselves to other fellowships—both churches and parachurch groups—as sympathetic Christian believers. Signs announcing their identity do not appear on Local Church properties. A person might attend Local Church meetings for months, unaware of any organizational ties to Witness Lee's church in Anaheim, California.

Witness Lee's Anaheim headquarters house two separate branches of the organization, both legally incorporated. Lee is technically and legally not the head of the first branch, the Local Church, which he serves as a salaried, official consultant. The second legal structure, called the Living Stream, Inc., is the ministry over which Witness Lee actually presides.

The ministry directed by Lee includes Stream Publications, which distributes Lee's many books, pamphlets and articles to an international readership. The ministry also distributes videotapes and tape recordings of Lee's presentations and lecture series. It also sponsors two ten-day training sessions each year in Los Angeles, attended by some 3,000 followers who pay fifty dollars per person. The Stream ministry receives nearly $750,000 annually.

Though Witness Lee is not legally at the helm of the Local Church organization, the presence and influence he wields there are equivalent to his presence and influence within the Stream ministry. Hence the two agencies are considered synonymous for the purposes of this book's theological and social commentary.

Besides the two agencies for ministry, Witness Lee and other Local Church figures have also engaged in two business enterprises called Day Star and Fosforus. Lee has served as chairman of the board of both companies. His son, Timothy Lee, has served as president of Fosforus.

Day Star of California sold motor homes until the fall of 1975, when, having failed to maintain a subsistence level of sales, it registered as a suspended operation. Fosforus was a Taiwan-based factory that initially manufactured parts for the Day Star recreation vans. When the California enterprise folded, Fosforus began to make chairs which Local Church congregations and individual members were encouraged to purchase for meeting halls and homes. A sufficient market was not created, however, and Fosforus then embarked on the manufacture of tennis rackets. (Although in the past Witness Lee had condemned all sports, the game of tennis is now exempt from his censure.) When that phase of operation also failed, Fosforus suspended operations but maintained its ninety-nine-year lease on its property. An unregistered agency, Overseas Christian Steward, acts as the parent body for both nonfunctioning corporations.

In another financial operation, funds solicited from Local Church members for a meeting hall in Stuttgart, Germany, were diverted into American real estate. The $235,000 collected was withdrawn from German banks in the spring of 1978 because of their low 3 per cent interest rate and invested in a six-apartment building located next to Witness Lee's home in Anaheim, California. Although that investment is appreciating, no apparent action has been taken to acquire the proposed Stuttgart meeting hall.

Recent Events
In the autumn of 1978 a significant split occurred in Local Church headquarters: more than forty members of the Anaheim congregation withdrew, including two of Lee's top administrators. Around the nation, several hundred others have followed their example, opting for a more consistently

biblical view of life and faith. Incensed Local Church elders, under Witness Lee's direction, have held special meetings for national and international leaders on how to deal with the defectors, particularly Max Rapoport, Lee's erstwhile heir apparent and former president of the Anaheim Local Church. From the "Max Conference" have stemmed rumors that Rapoport has been in league with the devil and is the betrayer Judas. In November 1978, however, Ron Kangas refused to acknowledge any attrition, describing the Anaheim dissidents as engaged in Local Church endeavors outside the Los Angeles vicinity. The Local Church has since responded to the defections by publishing a pamphlet entitled *The Belief and Practices of the Local Churches,* hoping to dispel any derogatory publicity. According to former members, however, the pamphlet, which is couched in evangelical language, accurately represents neither the beliefs nor practices of the Local Church.

The Local Church is now at a critical point in its history. The group cannot ignore external challenges and internal strife. Local Church leaders can respond to biblical challenges with the same kind of repentance expressed by the members who have withdrawn from Anaheim and other congregations. Or they can become more authoritarian, bringing pressures to bear which will effectively stifle internal controversy, but which will also insure continuing conflict with the greater Christian community.

3

Local Church Doctrine

"Feel me, See me, Touch me . . ."–Rock opera Tommy

Witness Lee's theology is based on human sensation. The predominant source of authority for his teachings and policies is the experience of internal impressions. Such impressions are accepted as trustworthy because they are assumed to be produced by the indwelling Holy Spirit. Indeed, the major thrust of Lee's ministry is to help believers act on the basis of impulses and sensations generated by God in the human spirit. Through them, he teaches, Christians gain knowledge of God. Authority for decision making in matters of life and faith, both great and small, stems from such sensations.

Sensuous Theology as the Source of Doctrine
Lee's theology is a sensuous theology. The Local Church

pointedly refers to spirituality and knowledge of God in terminology drawn from the world of the five physical senses: members are exhorted to "sense," "taste," "touch," "feel," "drink" and "eat" the God who indwells the human spirit. One immediate effect of that emphasis is to shift the basis of authority away from God's objective verbal revelation and toward personal, internal illumination. Lee seems to regard the Bible as a pointer, a manual of limited value, showing the general direction of faith and doctrine. The Bible does not, in Lee's thought, provide an ultimate authority for practice or behavior because it is a reference source external to the human spirit.

Sensuous theology is a theology of subjectivity. In it, knowledge of God is confined to an impulse of sensations within the human spirit; the authority for any understanding of God is derived from the "self-ish" subjective inner experiences of the individual Christian. The subjectivism of that kind of theology is exemplified by Lee's conviction that knowledge of God is neither communicable nor definable in clear, simple language. Knowledge of God and of his will is experiential, "sensational" and beyond the competence of language to convey. Lee's writings and teachings rely extensively on complex phraseology and literary devices like hyperbole and metaphor. Lee admits that his teaching is difficult to understand. Without objective knowledge, of course, the traditional categories of "biblical faith" and "biblical conduct" have little meaning.

For Witness Lee, spiritual experience is neither framed nor evidenced in categories of faith, obedience, growth in exercising spiritual gifts, or piety. Lee encourages his disciples toward an experience of God living in the human spirit whereby the mind's purpose and function is to intuit, feel and sense what God is generating through the spirit. "The Lord makes known His will to us mostly by way of our inner feeling; He seldom uses words."[1] Lee seems to search for

Scripture passages to justify his spiritual experiences, rather than letting all of Scripture judge those experiences.

In commentaries on the Old and New Testaments, Lee encourages the "inexpressible" spiritual experience. In his Old Testament commentaries, Lee ignores or even derides certain passages—those "pericopes" (as scholars call them) that speak of spirituality in relationship to the Law, piety and good works.[2] Conversely, he often allegorizes simple historical narratives, molding them to fit his sensuous theology.

In Witness Lee's theological system, spirituality transcends moral and ethical categories. It is related to ethics on only a secondary level. An ethic of "principle" is a practical and common concern among the unsanctified, Lee observes. The quality of spiritual union with God, according to Lee, is based more on the common sharing and mingling of human and divine essences than on an amity resulting from obedience to the ethical requirements prescribed in Scripture. That union, therefore, is expressed by a mystical, sensuous theology, not by propositional theology. Propositional theology presupposes that God has chosen language as a prime vehicle through which to communicate truth about life and faith. A favorite emphasis of Lee's is that Local Church members have the superior "subjective Christ"; other Christians have only an inferior "objective Christ."

Lee's Theological Method and Where It Leads

The "sense of God" in the human spirit is Witness Lee's principal didactic resource. His method for collating and organizing such "sensed" information employs unusual and complex theological structures pertaining to experience and sensation. The primacy Lee gives to experience in organizing biblical ideas creates several problems. Two of his theological procedures are particularly noticeable to someone trained in careful exegesis (proper interpretation) of Scripture. First, Lee often divorces similar, intimately related biblical ideas from one another, rather than distinguishing between their special emphases. Second, Lee often interpolates extrabiblical events or ideas into Scripture, thus tending to "canonize" his own views.

For Lee, the grammar and vocabulary of biblical authors carry theological constructs that parallel actual sense experiences or describe what sense experiences may be like. Each "sense-oriented" word of Scripture is critical, bearing its own singular significant meaning and connotation. In the usual method of interpretation, on the other hand, synonyms or closely related words are not readily divorced from each other. Biblical scholars such as Bernard Ramm,[3] Milton Terry[4] and Berkeley Mickelsen[5] recognize that choices of similar words frequently indicate distinctions, subtleties and emphases, rather than separations of ideas or uniform differences of meaning. Witness Lee, who does not employ that kind of hermeneutic (principle of interpretation), often forces unwarranted separations between theological constructs. For example, the complete separations of spirit and soul, faith and knowledge, God's life and God's nature, "flesh" and "the old man," sin and error, and biblical goodness and spiritual goodness are integral to Lee's theology (see Appendix 2).

Lee at times embellishes the scriptural records by interpolating into them some idea particularly consistent with the tenets of sensuous theology. Scholars use the term "eisegesis" for supposedly finding in Scripture something not actually there. Lee's eisegesis is notable in his discussions of the Genesis accounts of the creation and Fall. For example, although Adam was declared "very good" in God's sight (implying completeness), Lee concludes that Adam was not perfect. In Lee's interpretation, Adam lacked the life of God within him. That deficiency, according to Lee, enabled Satan literally to enter into the bodies of Adam and Eve at the instant of their disobedience. Lee also interpolates his ideas into the book of Romans, constructing from the grammar there three laws, each one regulating a different member of a person's tripartite composition.

To review our definition, a sensuous theology is a belief system focusing on one's experience of God, life and so forth, through attention to one's subjective, emotional and intuitional affections. A direct consequence of such a theology is that biblical concepts relevant to church life and social concerns (which necessarily extend beyond one's inner experience) are relegated to a position of secondary importance, if not negated altogether.

Witness Lee's most prolific period of writing was the period of the "greening of America," 1968 to 1973. As a resident of southern California, Lee was aware of the transitions in Western culture generated by the advent of the Beatles, the Vietnam War, campus protest rallies, "Jesus freaks," political skepticism and the redefinition of morality. Although an intelligent understanding of the shifts in society was crucial to Local Church growth and expansion, Lee chose not to address any of those concerns in his major publications.

Failure to exercise a social voice is representative of what Os Guinness has called the "mechanists and mystics" foible.[6] Such failure often indicates a split in mentality whereby life is divided into two nonintersecting, totally unrelated functions: the holy and the secular. In such a schema the secular lacks intrinsic value, and the sacred addresses only "religious" issues. Witness Lee concentrates exclusively on inner personal experience.

According to Guinness, one result of the sacred-secular split is that the organization of culture—its institutions and morality—is determined by "mechanists," people interested in determining the direction of society. On the other hand, "mystics," those who derogate external life circumstances to focus exclusively on internal spiritual experiences, are virtually noncontributors to the social momentum of culture;

hence they are vulnerable to oppression by mechanistic legislation. Local Church policy is to care for the poor and needy solely within their membership.[7] Having no external social consciousness or action, the Local Church is thus a body of mystics as defined above.

Witness Lee occasionally refers to certain authors who, as his mentors, serve to bolster and endorse elements of his teaching. Madame Guyon, a seventeenth-century French mystic, provides a supreme model for Lee of one who lived out the inner spiritual experience. Watchman Nee is also a key resource for Lee's repeated references to inner mystical experience. Reportedly, Lee has a number of Watchman Nee's unpublished manuscripts which serve as a springboard for his instruction of the Local Church.

Reality: Plato Revisited

Ontological Schism. Permeating all of Lee's teaching is an *ontological schism* (see Glossary). That is, his view of "reality and existence" posits two distinct levels of being. The two levels are regarded as separate and antagonistic to each other. They are mutually exclusive, interacting only when a mystical experience occurs.

"Reality" for Lee is different from our perception of the ordinary world. It is similar to the *Ideas* of Platonic philosophy (see Glossary) in which ultimate, real forms project an umbra or shadow on an already shadowy world existence. Lee's Reality also reflects the Gnostic concept of *Mind* in which the spirit world is exalted but the material world is considered profane. "What is truth? Do not think that truth means doctrine. The word 'truth' in such a passage [1 Timothy 3:15] means *reality*. Nothing is real in the whole universe, nothing is truth; everything is but a shadow. Everything that can be seen, everything that can be touched, everything that can be possessed and enjoyed is not real, but at best a shadow. Whatever exists in this universe is but a shadow, not the real thing."[8] In the same passage, Lee describes Christ as the "real thing," based on 1 John 5:12. Earthly food and even human life—its affections and history —are merely shadows, whereas Christ alone is real life.

Surprisingly, Lee leaves the attributes of his ultimate Reality (God) unspecified. Likewise, the qualities of the spiritual person are stated in vague general terms.[9] In contrast, "the soulish man" is described in detail.

For Lee, Reality, although objectively indescribable in common language, is subjectively attainable through experience. Reality is the spiritual substance casting the "shadows" which flicker about us in the form of the concrete material world. Thus, although history is a play of insubstantial and inconsequential appearances, by touching the higher spiritual Reality we may experience inwardly the substance which casts those shadows into the objective realm. "There are actually only two kinds of knowledge: the outward knowledge and the inward knowledge. To know the doings and the ways of God are both knowledge of an outward nature. . . . Yet to know God Himself is knowledge of an inward kind. This kind of knowledge comes as we touch God Himself by His life within and thereby know Him in a subjective and inward way."[10]

Epistemological Schism. So how does one know Reality? Corresponding to his ontological schism, Lee posits an *epistemological schism* (see Glossary). That is, his view of knowledge includes two distinct ways of knowing. The first way, spiritual knowledge, like Reality, is ineffable. It is outside the realm of rationality and is related to some kind of inner experience.

The worship services of the Local Church bear out how completely they have cut themselves off from the objective realm. Whenever they encounter the word "truth" (such as in John 1:17), they automatically substitute the word "reality." Likewise, "grace" is exchanged for "enjoy-

ment." Frequent testimonies tell of how some are still be-
set by the habit of trying to understand what they read
due to "the poison of education," but how God is deliver-
ing them and helping them to "just eat the Word." Another excitedly testified of pray-reading backwards and
experiencing great joy because "it's all God's Word and
when you touch any part of it you touch God." Other frequent exclamations include: "The Book is not the words
of God, but the Word of God"; "We don't come to it for
knowledge, but for the Person"; "We don't try to get something out of the Word, but to get the Word into us." One
youth testified that he faced a special temptation of Satan
and began to look for a passage of Scripture to help him.
Then his spirit convicted him and reminded him to just
"Amen" the words of his quiet time passage, "So I just
'Amened' the word 'pomegranates' and my faith was released and Satan defeated."[11]

Once one knows the Real, how can one communicate it?
Witness Lee's answer is obscure. Since Reality is outside the
realm of logic, tight arguments will not convey what is intended. "We need not argue with others; we should just bear
Christ and sometimes blow the trumpet. Blowing the trumpet means giving the testimony. If someone argues, just
praise the Lord. The more they try to condemn you, the more
you should give the testimony and praise the Lord."[12]

Ordinary, consistent word usage and grammar are likewise dispensable. If Reality is entirely otherworldly, no
mere words can adequately convey it or contain it. Why even
try to be linguistically precise? The Local Church can use the
same words as orthodox Christianity, but without the same
meanings.[13]

The second way of knowing in Lee's epistemological
schism concerns the temporal world. Rational thoughts and
understanding are restricted to the world. Coupled with
direct perception of that world with the five human senses,

they are the basis for knowing the realm of shadows.

Spiritual Authority: Feeling One's Way

The problem of authority (its source and who wields it) is a significant test for healthy communities. Although Witness Lee decries church hierarchies, their forms and written constitutions, the Local Church is not a model of democracy. Lee's voice has always been far weightier in the organization than anyone else's. Reliable sources say that Lee rules with a firm hand. Exercising deference to all of Lee's requests, the inner circle serves as a model for the obedience and submission encouraged among Local Church congregations. Although the Local Church denies that Lee is an autocratic "pope" and claims that Scripture is their paramount authority, there is some reason for skepticism. Among Stream Publications, editions of Lee materials predominate, with minimal contributions from other Local Church figures. The non-Lee materials are generally apologetic, presenting a defense of Local Church positions in accordance with Lee's desires.

Although the Local Church publicly supports the supremacy and authority of Scripture, Witness Lee's persuasive argumentation and spirited theology provide the accepted interpretation of Scripture. Any attempt to exercise biblical leverage on questionable issues by a member of the Local Church is overruled by Lee's authoritative interpretation, irrespective of its accuracy.[14] It was that style of authority which prompted Max Rapoport to resign his post as president of the Local Church in Anaheim. In the *Los Angeles Times* (December 11, 1978), Rapoport was quoted as saying that he attempted to encourage the exercise of biblical discipline in a case of moral indiscretion on the part of Witness Lee's son Phillip. Discouraged by Lee from applying scriptural discipline, Rapoport was subsequently removed from Lee's graces and gradually lost his power and reputation.

A reputable source active in the Local Church for years says that Local Church people believe Witness Lee to be the only oracle of God alive today. To disagree with the oracle is tantamount to being out of the Holy Spirit's leading. "When I command in my spirit, the Lord commands with me, for I am one spirit with the Lord."[15] " . . . Is this my teaching? No! This is the revelation of God in the Bible. It was buried, it was covered for centuries, but by His mercy it has been discovered."[16] (This follows a discussion of the relation of daily lives to quality of worship, using 1 Corinthians as the text.)

Some Local Church people have privately confessed belief that Witness Lee is *the* apostle of this age. No spokesman for the executive branch of the Local Church has corrected that understanding, or tried to dissuade members from embracing that view. Lee himself believes that he stands in the line of the apostolic succession, his authority commensurate with that of the twelve apostles. Lee claims to have received the apostolic mantle from Watchman Nee during their last meeting, when Lee was commissioned to supervise the Taiwan churches.

A striking anecdote illustrates Witness Lee's view of the complete sufficiency of his apostleship. Lee once told an elder that the church was like a car; it has only one driver at any given moment. And, he went on, nobody appreciates a back-seat driver. Passengers should cover their eyes, close their mouths and never distract the driver. Lee demonstrated proper "passenger posture" by putting his hands over his eyes and mouth. During similar conversations Lee's climactic statement has been that, even if the car were headed for a cliff, driver and passengers alike should all go over the edge together.

Scripture: Does It Mean What It Says?
Because the epistemological schism affects Witness Lee's view of God's written Word, the Bible assumes a subsidiary

position in his theology. The words of Scripture have meanings, including references to certain facts and events of history, but meaning in general and factuality in particular have less significance for Lee than the personal, subjective experience of Christ in the human spirit.[17] That experience can be opened up to us through reading the Bible, but it occurs through a process of spiritual osmosis having nothing to do with understanding what we read.[18] The written Word is a shadow, not a reality. A higher nonrational spiritual Word exists behind the rational meaning of the written Word. The biblical data act like an erratic compass rather than a definitive guide to reality.

Commenting on Romans 2:29 and 7:6, where the apostle Paul wrote that Christians are released from the law (the "letter"), Lee writes: "Now we know what the word 'letter' here refers to—it is the written Bible. Today we must serve the living Lord with newness in the spirit, not according to the oldness of the written Bible. . . . Everyone must admit that the word 'letter' in these passages refers to the written Scriptures. There can be no argument."[19]

Inspiration. As a result of downgrading propositional revelation (the view that spiritual truths can be communicated in language comprehended by the human mind), Lee embraces a faulty view of the inspiration of Scripture. In discussing the psalms and their emphasis on the emotive experience of God, Lee distinguishes between psalms that champion the virtues of righteous behavior according to the law and those that advance the virtues of possessing the Spirit of God in the human spirit. In Lee's opinion, the former are peculiarities, expressions of men who did not experience a full spiritual transformation in their lives.

Throughout his writings, Lee systematically derides keeping the law as inferior to possessing God's life. "You're into Psalm One" is a comment railed against Local Church members who seek to apply ethical standards derived from the written laws of Scripture to their daily lives. Holiness and righteousness resulting from obedience to the precepts and commandments of God reflect a less spiritual condition than simply possessing God's Spirit. Consequently, Lee says that psalms emphasizing the law are humanly rather than divinely inspired. Below is a diagram of his position.[20]

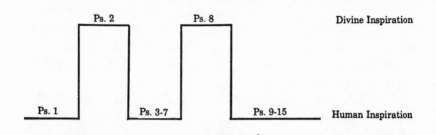

To Witness Lee, we are released from obligations to revere the *written* Bible because of its shadowy inferiority. The true Bible is the person of the Holy Spirit. The presence of the Holy Spirit is the ultimate reality. His presence is not clearly or sufficiently expressed through the vehicle of written language.

What is the substance, the essence of God's Word? The answer is found in II Timothy 3:16, "All Scripture is God-breathed...." The King James Version says "given by inspiration of God," but the meaning in the original language is *God-breathed*. All Scripture is God's breath. We know that God is Spirit (John 4:24); the Spirit is God's essence and nature.... Since the Word is the breath of God, and God is Spirit, whatever is breathed out of God must be Spirit! So the essence or nature of the Word of God is Spirit. It is not just a thought, revelation, teaching, or doctrine, but Spirit. The Spirit is the very substance of the Word of God.... The nature of this book is the very essence of God Himself....

... What is it? We must look at the Word of God as recorded in Ephesians 6:17-18. To make verse 17 clearer, it is better to add a word which is absolutely correct according to the grammatical construction of the original language. We can translate it in this way: "Take ye ... the sword of the Spirit, which Spirit is the Word of God." It is the Spirit that is the Word of God.[21]

Lee's notion of a dual level of Scripture's inspiration means that he must incessantly editorialize on the difference between the humanly inspired and the God-breathed.

Textual Manipulation. The grand illusion of Witness Lee's *Christ versus Religion* is the view that Jesus completely rejected the religion of the Old Testament. By manipulating the biblical data, Lee subtly links both liberal and conservative Christian camps to the New Testament Pharisees who espoused the Old Testament traditions. That stratagem disconcertingly persuades readers that Jesus, while rejecting liberal and conservative Christians, heartily approves of and rejoices over the Local Church. To pave the way for that conclusion, Lee must manipulate the historical data in the Gospel records.

Concerning John the Baptist, for example, Lee writes: "John acted in a way radically opposed to religion.... He had no religion,... he was versus religion,... he said nothing about the ten commandments. He gave that up."[22] Lee disregards the fact that John was jailed and ultimately beheaded because he exhorted the guilty, vindictive king, Herod Antipas, with the seventh commandment, "Thou shalt not commit adultery." Later, Lee writes of Jesus: "In those days there was the holy place, the holy temple, the holy city, and the holy land—a four-fold holy sphere. Jesus kept himself away from every one of them."[23]

Why should Lee write in such a hyperbolic fashion and make such an extreme assertion, when it is clear from the Gospel records that Jesus was circumcised according to the

law, taught in the holy temple and kept feasts in the holy
city? Lee finds it expedient to subordinate the data of the
written Word in order to validate his charges against non-
Local Church Christianity and to substantiate his sensuous
theology. Lee manipulates texts describing the Pharisees
in an identical way: "They are violently opposed to Jesus. . . .
They not only opposed Him, but even attempted to kill Him.
. . . These were not sinful people; neither were they what we
think of as worldly people; they were religious, and they
were for God. . . . The situation is the very same today. The
more we live by Jesus, . . . the more the religious people will
hate us."[24]

Lee's appraisal contradicts Jesus' declaration in Matthew
23 that a pharisaical mind-set is sinful, secular and antagonistic to God and his plan of redemption. Lee distorts Scripture in this case to validate the parallel he draws between
the "religious" Pharisees of Christ's day and contemporary
Christians. "What is it to be religious? . . . simply to be
sound, scriptural, and fundamental, yet without the presence of Christ."[25]

According to Lee, only through alignment with the Local
Church can one be truly in Christ's presence. The testimony
of Christians outside the Local Church, however, is that one
cannot be "sound, scriptural and fundamental" apart from
Christ.

For Witness Lee the written Word is not revelation; it
only contains revelation for those who can see through its
shadowy words. Where, then, is the immutable standard
for authoritatively interpreting the Bible? The traditional
reference point of biblical Christianity—"Scripture interprets Scripture"—has been relocated by Lee. "Our spirit
today is God's dwelling place. And, even more, the local
churches are God's dwelling place. Hence, we must turn to
our spirit, and we must turn to the local church. . . . Our spirit and the local church are the places where we will receive

divine revelation, where we obtain the explanation to all our problems."[26]

The written Word is not entirely written off by Lee, however. Although it is a shadow it can lead to Reality. To help his followers use it, Lee presents a number of interpretive principles in his books.[27] Two stand out: allegory and personal revelation.

Some of Lee's books are structured entirely by the allegorical use of Scripture. For him, almost everything in the Old Testament is a symbol of something in the New Testament. Obviously, if one views the written Word and history as shadows, then to span one's ontological schism to the higher spiritual Reality behind the shadows requires something other than literal interpretation.

Similarly, if one sees ordinary knowledge as outward, "soulish" and crass, one cannot use rational, verbal, objective knowing to span the epistemological schism and attain spiritual knowledge. Lee says we need an existential and personal revelation; the Bible is revelation only if we keep on seeing through its shadowy words and concepts. Since language and history are of the mind, of the soul, of the lower level of knowing, such matters as the Bible's grammar and the original historical context and intent are inconsequential to Lee.[28]

Lee teaches that Scripture is the Holy Spirit and that the interpretation of Scripture is spiritual, beyond rational understanding. If we think, he says, we are only in trouble.[29] To use the Bible, he says, what we need is some exuberant shouting—the fire that burns the mind away. "If you stay with the Bible for half an hour or even an hour and get no fire, you are wrong. I can tell you, just after two minutes of, 'O Lord Jesus! In the beginning was the Word. Amen! O Lord Jesus, You are the Word! Amen, Lord Jesus! Hallelujah!' you will be burned. This is the right way to contact the Word."[30]

Lee further states that the words of Scripture are deadened if studied with the mind (i.e., with understanding). To exercise the spirit (i.e., calling on the Lord's name) when reading the Bible, however, vivifies the words of Scripture.[31] "Actually, the Bible is not principally for man to understand, but for man to receive and enjoy. . . . If you use your mind to analyze and comprehend the Bible, it is unavoidable that you will understand it wrongly, thus misinterpreting the words of the Lord."[32]

The Scriptures as Counsel. When people come to Witness Lee for counsel regarding the affairs of life and faith, he exhorts them to experience more of Christ—to seek a greater presence of God in the spirit, to "call on the name of the Lord" —rather than reforming their actions or thought life. "Sometimes they press me to tell them in detail how to live, how to get along, and how to deal with their wives. Then I tell them, 'Brother, I have told you clearly, Christ is the best way. . . . Forget about everything. Just come to the Lord in your spirit to have a personal contact with Him.' "[33]

Lee says that counsel from God comes through an inner, sensate experience of God, not through Scripture. In a similar vein, Lee writes: "Are you sorrowful? . . . Do not attempt to encourage yourself and overcome your problems. Bring all your sorrows to the local church. . . . If your wife is angry, just tell her, 'Dear, let us go to the church.' Don't try to solve your problems in your home and then come to the church. You will be frustrated. . . . I have had many experiences like this. As soon as I have come into the entrance of the meeting hall, the enemies and problems have fled."[34]

Consistently, Witness Lee's counsel steers parishioners away from biblical ethics regarding behavior and away from teachings which encourage responsibility and positive action. Paul's counsel to Timothy, cited earlier, heralds Scripture as being useful for teaching, rebuking, correcting and training in righteousness—a counsel that seems to lie dormant in Lee's sensuous theology. "The church is not a place for the education or correction of people. The church is not a place to change people."[35] Yet the Scripture says that "whatever was written in earlier times was written for our instruction, that through perseverance and the encouragement of the Scriptures we might have hope" (Rom. 15:4).

Witness Lee's general attitude toward Scripture is summed up in these words: "We need a spiritual understanding with the Scriptures opened in such a way that we see all the secrets behind the writings."[36]

God, Humanity and Salvation: Big Issues

An outstanding difference between Witness Lee's teaching and historical Christian orthodoxy is that Lee presents a flowing unity in his doctrines of God, humanity and salvation. The biblical doctrines can be treated separately, but with Lee's theological method it is difficult or impossible to distinguish among them. A sensuous theology, based on inner subjective experiences and unconditioned by the full implications of scriptural teaching, is confined to self-reflection. Lee's self-reflection, when contemplating the activities of the Trinity, biblical anthropology and salvation, yields a "saving mysticism" with humanity as the arbiter of meaning and with God and the cosmos integrated.

God. Although Local Church leaders in official statements "strongly reject any kind of association with modalism,"[37] modalistic thought often appears in Lee's writings.[38] On the other hand, trinitarian language is not absent from Lee's theology; in places he speaks of one unchangeable substance and of three persons. But his illustrations tend to be modalistic: the Father becomes the Son who becomes the Spirit. Lee says that the persons of the Trinity are actually "... three stages of one God. ... For example, ice becomes water, and water becomes vapor—one substance assumes three forms."[39]

Elsewhere Lee says that the three persons of the Trinity represent three successive steps in God's existence. Further, without those consecutive stages—the Trinity as Creator, Redeemer and Quickener—God could not have dispensed his essence into humanity.[40] Later in the same work, Lee writes that the individual members of the Triune God actuated the creation, in addition to participating corporately in Christ's Incarnation, death, resurrection, ascension and glorification.[41]

Lee's illustrations characteristically blur the distinction between God and the believer. Lee draws an analogy between a person's conversion and subsequent spiritual growth, and pouring grape juice into pure water. As the pure water becomes grape juice (i.e., its identity is completely absorbed), so our human nature is swallowed up and identified with God's nature when conversion is successful.[42]

In discussing God, and humanity's relation to God, Lee divides the being of God into distinct fragments rather than appreciating emphases or nuances in Scripture that characterize God's personality as a whole. "We have seen ... that in the life of God is contained the nature of God, and in the life of God is hidden the fullness of God; therefore the law contained in the life of God is compatible with God Himself, with what God is, and with the nature of God; hence, this law is the law of God Himself. When the life of God brings its law into us, this also means that it brings the law of God into us."[43]

Lee's building-block approach in the use of biblical terms may have taken him further than he would care to admit. The logical extension of the reasoning sketched above is that God (a single, indivisible Spirit according to John 4:24) is composed of parts. Would this not require a sort of God-beyond-God who could unify the fragments?

Witness Lee's attempt to elevate the significance of the Local Church also seems to influence his perception of God.

Lee says that even the nature of God is contingent upon God's foreknowledge of the church. "The full revelation of the Scripture reveals to us that all things in the universe are for the church. Even the three Persons of the Godhead are for the divine purpose of having a church to fulfill God's eternal plan."[44] And ". . . it is the desire and purpose of God's heart to secure a corporate man, . . . that He Himself may obtain eternal rest."[45] Lee's *unspoken* premise seems to be that if creation hadn't occurred, the Trinity would not exist; before the Fall, one might conclude, the Trinity was a non-entity. The *spoken* premise is that God's mode of existence depended on the formation of the human church.

One of Lee's unbiblical claims is that God needs Satan as well as humankind to complete his personality. "God is not sorry that there is such an evil one as Satan, because without such a one, God's manifold wisdom could not be manifested. . . . The whole universe has been damaged by Satan, but God needs such a one in order that His wisdom might be shown."[46]

According to Scripture, before the actual creation of the universe, God existed as the three self-sustaining persons of the Trinity, creatively relating to one another without needing fellowship from any outside source. Theologians call this the ontological Trinity (cf. Jn. 17:5). Witness Lee seems to confuse this with an "economic" Trinity (a Trinity that relates to creation as Father, Son and Holy Spirit), which in turn for Lee spawns the concept that God *needs* humanity and Satan.

Also according to Scripture, God has patterns of relating to the created order which are consonant with his character. The economy of salvation (see Glossary) that God designed engages each member of the Trinity uniquely, but with parity. Theology should never transfer values derived from the way God relates to creation either to God's character or to the relationships within the Trinity. For example, Christ's subordination to the Father during his earthly ministry does not imply inequality within the Godhead.

Yet from the fact that God relates to humankind in the context of a fallen world, Witness Lee seems to infer an imperfect God who requires the presence of humans and even an adversary, Satan, to authenticate himself. Lee is saying that without evil, God's goodness cannot be manifested. He also seems to be saying that without the true church (the Local Church), God cannot exist completely or purposefully.

Humanity. Witness Lee teaches that the nature of humanity, both fallen and newly redeemed, is tripartite: body, soul and spirit.[47] Soul and spirit in turn consist of three parts each. To Lee, human nature looks like this:

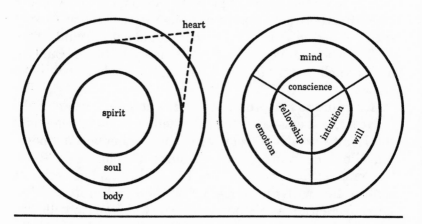

The *body* is our "outward parts," for *physical life.*

The *soul* is our "inward parts," for *expressing God;* it consists of mind, will and emotions.

The *spirit* is our "hidden parts," for *contacting, receiving* and *containing God;* it is composed of conscience, intuition and fellowship with God.

The *heart* is soul and spirit in proper relationship, for *loving God* with a unified personality.

Lee seldom speaks of the three component parts of human beings standing as a unified, integrated whole in positive relationship to God. For redeemed humanity, the body and soul are pitted antagonistically against the spirit, which is God's dwelling place. Hence, the body and soul can "box God in." The objective is for the protagonist (the human spirit) to subdue the antagonists (the body and soul) and establish a working relationship of spirit and soul. The result, however, is described in sensate terms: walking, eating, tasting, touching and so forth. Lee's ontological schism—segregation of a higher spiritual Reality from lower worldly shadows—is only partially bridged, never entirely resolved.

In Lee's teaching, the soul was the center of humankind before the Fall. The soul of unfallen Adam could not attain the fellowship with the Creator that God intended because Adam and Eve were imperfect; God did not implant his essence in them before their seduction by Satan.[48] Despite biblical references to humankind as the image of God, Lee derives from his reading of the Bible the idea that Adam necessarily required the life of God, the element of God or Holy Spirit, to "round him out." But Adam fell before receiving that "extra something," the Spirit. Lee's beliefs about the nature of humanity obviously affect his view of regeneration.

According to Lee, created humanity needed to be regenerated even without the actual, historical Fall. In his theology, untarnished *created* human nature is just as much a part of the "old creation" as is *fallen* human nature; it is incomplete, minus the life of God. "God's purpose for us human beings is that we may obtain His uncreated life and be transformed into His image to be like Him, as He is. Therefore, even if our human life had not been corrupted, we would still need to be regenerated."[49]

In his further interpretation of Genesis 1—3, Lee proposes that God did intend to live in humanity. Since human beings

were intended to contain and express God's essence, humankind ultimately becomes the center of the universe.[50] Humankind fell anyway. In Lee's interpretation of Scripture,
when Adam ate from the tree of the knowledge of good and
evil, he literally ingested Satan, who then grew in his body
and transformed it into "the flesh." Satan, the usurper of
God's authority, seduced Adam, but was unable to live in his
spirit. Thus Satan remains trapped in the *body*—merely one-
third of an individual's total constitution. "By the fall, Satan
came to dwell in our body, causing our body to become flesh
—i.e., a damaged, ruined body.... The body is something
satanic and devilish, because Satan dwells in this body....
Now you see that the fall of man was not just a matter of man
committing something against God, but of man *receiving
Satan into his body*. Satan, from the time of the fall, dwells
in man."[51]

Though the spirit is dead (i.e., not functioning), it is not
eradicated or possessed.[52] According to Lee, the human spirit was intended to be the dwelling place of God's life because Adam was to eat from the tree of life—"to ingest"
God—and thus possess the divine Spirit in his finite spirit.
In both regenerate and unregenerate people Satan indwells
the body, the self governs the soul, and God indwells the
spirit, the factions mutually exclusive of one another and
characteristically working at cross-purposes.

The Savior. Both the created and fallen natures of humanity need drastic changes: they need a savior. Therefore, according to Lee, the Father became the Son. That is, in some
sense the person of the Father was united with the person of
the Son in the Incarnation. Lee argues for the union of
divine persons from Isaiah 9:6, John 10:30 and John 14:7-11.
"This is Wonderful! The One is really two! He is the Son as
well as the Father!... This word [John 14:8-9] indicates
clearly that the Son is the Father. Yet some twist this word
saying the Son is not the Father, but the representative of

the Father. This is twisting. If you read the context without any twisting, you can realize the Son was the Father there."[53]

Lee's modalistic presentation of the Trinity might cause one to ask, "Then who died on the cross?" Lee deviates from traditional Christology also in his understanding of the divine and human nature of Christ. Lee's incarnate deity was neither quite God nor quite man; he was a third entity, a "mingled" God-man.

"Mingling" is a term of historical orthodoxy once used to describe the relation of humanity and divinity in the person of Christ. The term was also used, although rarely, to describe humankind's relationship to God. Both uses were eventually discarded because they were judged inadequate or too imprecise to express those relationships.[54] Witness Lee, however, has chosen to resurrect and employ the term. His usage of it illustrates why historically it was displaced by more adequate terms. Early in the pages of *The God of the Resurrection,* Lee speaks of the "dual nature" in Christ, which could represent the orthodox view that Christ's two natures comprised one personality.[55] Later it becomes clear that by a dual nature Lee means "combining the natures of God and man" to produce one syncretistic new nature. "Therefore, the incarnation of Christ simply means the mingling of God with humanity. Mingling is much more than mixing together; it is an intrinsic union.... Do you realize why He is so precious to us? Because in Him is the universal mingling of God with humanity."[56]

Witness Lee says that the mingled God-man lived in order to die for three purposes.[57] The least important purpose was judgment of sin, of the Fall. At the Fall, Satan was fooled. He did not expect to be trapped within humans; he saw them only as food. But humans were also bait, and Satan was caught and imprisoned in them. Therefore, when Christ put on human nature, he also put on Satan, and when Christ died, Satan (who was trapped within him) also was put to death.[58]

Another purpose of Christ's death, in Lee's theology, was the killing of the old creation—all of the old creation. Human nature is part of the old creation, according to Lee. At Christ's crucifixion, humanity and Satan and his thralldom were also crucified; the world, sin and the "old man" met their end. Lee exhorts his followers to experience this all-inclusive death wherein the entire old creation has been crucified.[59]

The most important purpose of Christ's death was the impartation of life to human beings through the mingling of God with them. Even if humankind had never sinned, Christ would still have had to die for humanity—just as any kind of food must die before being eaten, just as Adam had to be put to sleep before Eve became a living creature.[60] "Even if we were not sinful, Christ still must die for us. He had to die that He might be our life-supply."[61] Witness Lee anticipates our question: "Perhaps you ask, Why did God put all things to death in Christ and then later bring all things to resurrection in Him? The answer is foreign to our thinking. At creation, nothing of God Himself was mingled with the creature. If we search the Scriptures, we must conclude that at the time of creation man did not receive the life of God. Nothing of God was mingled with man. But through the death and resurrection of Christ, God mingled Himself with man!"[62]

Theological Antinomy. Antinomy (from the Greek *anti,* against, and *nomos,* law) refers to apparent contradiction or inconsistency between two laws or principles that seem to be mutually exclusive. Witness Lee claims that after Christ died, he arose and became the Spirit, a new Spirit. For Lee, references to the Spirit in John 14 are actually about the crucified and resurrected Christ.[63] Lee favors the phrase, "the Lord Spirit," to describe this unity of divine persons. The new Spirit is everything that Jesus Christ is. "The Person of the Lord Jesus is the Holy Spirit. The Holy Spirit is just the Lord Himself (II Cor. 3:17). He Himself is the life-giving Spirit (I Cor. 15:45). So, the Holy Spirit, as the Person of the Lord, is the reality of the Lord's name."[64] "Included in the Spirit of Jesus today are the divine nature and the human nature. Today, the Holy Spirit of Christ is such an all-inclusive Spirit! It is this Holy Spirit, the Spirit with both the divine and human nature, that unites the saints together."[65]

This Spirit is new, not the Spirit of God referred to in the Old Testament. "We must realize that the Holy Spirit in the New Testament is different from the Spirit of God in the Old Testament. The Spirit of God in the Old Testament was only of one element, divinity, because He was solely the Spirit of God. But the Holy Spirit today in the New Testament is of many elements, including the divine nature, the human nature, the effectiveness of Christ's death, and the power of His resurrection."[66]

After the cross, only the "eternal Spirit" remains. Everything else was terminated. Even the Trinity is now in the Spirit. This Lord, who seems to be both three persons and one person, both human and divine, is now the God of our salvation. "Today the Lord whom we enjoy is that Spirit (II Cor. 3:17), and that Spirit is the very Triune God. . . . In this Spirit there is God, and in this Spirit there is also man."[67]

In "this Spirit" Lee also includes the (Local) Church, so the three modes of divine appearance that comprise the Triune Godhead acquire a new appendage! "They are now four in one: the Father, the Son, the Spirit, and the Body."[68] In view of such teaching, many will wonder how Local Church leaders could claim publicly that they "believe in the Trinity as it has been understood in traditional Catholic and Protestant circles."[69] One answer is simply that Local Church thinking accommodates contradictions without difficulty, as has already been observed.

Any attempt to demystify the biblical Trinity is replete
with problems, as Lee's words evidence:

> ... a man full of purpose may have several appearances.
> If you could visit him at his home in the early hours of the
> day, you would see that he is a father or a husband. After
> breakfast, he may go to a university to be a professor.
> Then at the hospital in the afternoon, you may see him in
> a white uniform as a doctor. At home he is a father, in the
> university he is a professor, and in the hospital he is a doc-
> tor. Why is he these three kinds of persons? Because he is a
> man of great purpose.
>
> Do not think that because there are three Persons in the
> Godhead, there are three separate Gods. No, they are ab-
> solutely one. ... The father in the home, the professor in
> the university, and the doctor in the hospital are also
> three persons with one name.[70]

One critic points out: "This father, professor, and doctor is
not three persons; he is one person only. Father, professor,
and the doctor are merely three functions of one person, but
in no way are they distinct persons. So it is with the Local
Church 'Trinity.' They can call the Father, Son, and Spirit
persons, but it is meaningless when they redefine the
term."[71] Rather than identifying Lee as a strict modalist, the
above illustration indicates the inability of language completely to resolve and explain antinomy. Light is described
by physicists as being both a particle and a wave, an example of antinomy. Christians describe the Trinity as being
both three persons and one God, another antinomy. Theologically, Lee seems to broaden that antinomy, believing
in both a modalistic God and a trinitarian God. Most of
Lee's critics categorize him as a modalist, based on writings
in which he clearly takes a modalistic view. More accurately,
one should take note of Lee's peculiar, unbiblical antinomy
that insists on a "three-and-one" God: a Triune God who is
modalistic as well as trinitarian.

Salvation. Salvation is of the Spirit in Witness Lee's theology. As God became a new thing in some sense, becoming the "Lord Spirit," so human beings become a new thing, a historical novelty. Just as Christ became a God-man by the mingling of his divinity with humanity, human beings become "God-men" by the mingling of their spirits with God the Spirit. It could be said that people are not so much redeemed as they are replaced. The crux of Local Church teaching seems to be that God is working himself into people and at times even replacing them with himself. "Do you know what it means to be a real Christian? To be a Christian simply means to be mingled with God, to be a God-man."[72]

The function of salvation is primarily to effect (or permit) that mingling, not to atone for sin. Although Witness Lee acknowledges the redemptive aspect of salvation, he explicitly labels it the "lower aspect." The "higher aspect" of salvation is the mingling of God's essence with the essence of humankind: Lee literally devotes volumes to its explication. The imparting of divine life to human beings has virtually nothing to do with the forgiveness of sin. Regeneration would have been necessary even if Adam had not fallen. "If God desired man to be only a good man, and man had not fallen and been corrupted, he would not need to be regenerated. But God's desire is not that man should be only a good man, but, much more, a GOD-man, one who is the same as He is."[73]

For Lee, atonement deals primarily with the corrupted body, the flesh, in which Satan is incarnated. The soul, according to Lee, does not need to be redeemed except insofar as it is wedded to the flesh. The human spirit, on the other hand, is quickened (when God comes into a person by means of the mingling of the divine and human spirits). Since God is Spirit, whatever he begets is Spirit, "the very substance of Himself."[74]

Redeemed Humanity: Tetrapartite. In Witness Lee's theology, the goal of regeneration is a redeemed (quickened) humanity, a brand new creature in some way spiritually "consubstantial" (one in substance) with God. Recall Lee's definition of mingling: "Mingling is much more than mixing together; it is an intrinsic union."[75] Elsewhere Lee teaches that the once separate human and divine natures are now fused into one unit.[76] "The church's beauty is not in anything but the divine nature. She is royal and she is divine."[77] "The Father is in the Son, the Son is in the Spirit, and the Spirit is in the Body. They are now four in one: the Father, the Son, the Spirit and the Body."[78] Lee seems to see God's existence as a tetrapartite (four-part) complex, three parts divine and one part human, all existing on the same plane of value. Lee sees no difference between the essence of quickened humanity and the essence of the Triune Spirit. How could there be? The two have become one, the spirit in humans becoming at least semi-divine. Comparing quickened humanity to the nature of Christ, Lee makes such statements as these: "What He is, we are; and what we are, He is."[79] "After some time, Christ to a certain extent becomes this man. . . . he and Christ become one."[80] Relative to the Spirit, as well as to Christ, quickened humanity has become a unity.

Lee's proposal that God's Spirit and the believer's spirit are mingled together to create one spirit resolves any difficulties encountered by Bible translators in determining whether "spirit" in certain passages refers to the human spirit or to the Holy Spirit.[81] Relative to God, quickened humanity is the same substance (essence). "The very essence of the almighty, all-inclusive, universal God is simply Spirit. God is the Manufacturer, and He intends to reproduce Himself as the Product; therefore, whatever He reproduces must be Spirit, the very substance of Himself."[82] In many passages, Witness Lee declines to differentiate between the creature and Creator. Typically, he asserts that believers possess the life of God, which enables them to be as God is and to do what God does.[83]

Yet two wars are going on inside a believer. One war is like a schizophrenia. The quickened person's personality is no longer in the soul but in the spirit, although the old soul-ish nature lives on. The other war is a three-cornered struggle: Satan is still in the flesh as sin, God is mingled in with the human spirit, and the self is still in the soul.[84] Lee regards the believer as a miniature garden of Eden. The three original parties in the historic garden of Eden—God, Adam and Satan—indwell the believer. God possesses the spirit; Adam resides in the soul (self); Satan lodges in the body. God and Satan are engaged in continuous battle from their respective bases of operation within an individual.[85]

For Witness Lee, one's victory over Satan and self is won mystically. When one is in the spirit, one is in heaven, in the "Holiest of all," and somehow heaven can flow out. The epistemological schism is not healed by salvation; rather, salvation enables one to jump to the upper level, the level of ineffable, irrational, inner knowledge.

Likewise, the ontological schism endures. The redeemed ones are graced with lofty experiences of Reality, and that Reality (named Christ) has analogues in the shadowy realm of matter and history. "This must be all the items of what Christ is. As God, He is the Father, the Son, the Spirit, the Lord, the Christ and other items. As man, Christ is the Apostle, the Teacher, the Leader, etc. He is really much more than all this. He is the light, the life, the air, the water, the food, the clothing and the lodging."[86]

Sanctification: The Magical Mystical Tour
Sensuous theology finds a major point of departure from orthodox theology in the subjective experience of God within the individual. Witness Lee's most detailed theological concern is in the area of sanctification. Progressive sanctification is for Lee a process whereby one can obtain a "bigger

and better" possession of God. Lee's constant exhortations to sanctification, however, and his explanations of how it comes about, have an elusive vagueness about them. Since common descriptive language is incapable of capturing the experience of God, Lee's writings employ such literary devices as poetry, hyperbole, illustrative storytelling and embellishment of biblical narratives.

Although Lee has written volumes on the subject of sanctification, his basic steps for Christian growth appear to be simple. The mingled divine-human spirit "releases" new life into the soul (self) and body (satanic) after "killing" the body-soul complex. The new man in the spirit must overcome the old man in the soul. The God of redemption indwelling the spirit must overcome the created self lodged in the soul, removing it from the influence of Satan who inhabits the body. Lee's catch phrase for that process is "the breaking of the outer man."

In Lee's concept, if the division between soul and spirit (see Heb. 4:12) is not sensually registered in the Christian's daily experience, sanctification means nothing. Failure to experience that distinction means that the old self persists in the body-soul complex, and that God remains imprisoned in the human spirit. But once the division is experienced, the self and the body-soul complex are "killed" by the divine-human Spirit-spirit's passing through the heart and engaging in victorious battle with the soul. The "released" soul then floats up to "touch" the Spirit which subdues it, whereby the process of sanctification can begin. That process produces a two-way communication between Reality and the human being. That going up/coming down, passing to and from shadow (body-soul) and Reality (Spirit-spirit) is difficult. Lee admits that few people manage to effect it consistently.[87]

Killing. "Killing" is Witness Lee's term for the initial, negative, quelling phase of the sanctification process. The archenemy to be slain is the soul. Wedded to the sinful flesh, the soul's primary need is not to be redeemed but to be "subdued," so that it can be wedded to the mingled divine-human spirit. The soul is then the secondary member of a union whose value is totally contingent on the dominance of the mingled spirit. "As long as I experience the Holy Spirit moving and working within me, I will sense the killing of my desires, my intentions, my habits, my character, etc. The more I am filled with the Holy Spirit, the more I will be killed, for within the Spirit of Jesus Christ is the effective killing element of Christ's death."[88]

Nothing from the soul can be spiritual; the soul cannot desire God or receive things from God.[89] In Lee's view, Christians should initially *sense* forgiveness, then grasp it with the mind. They should *sense* God's presence rather than *believe* it.

Lee claims that when the soul is denied, the *life* of the soul (the self, the ego) is put to death, but the *faculties* (mind, will, emotion) still operate—without a soulish self. The faculties will be used as instruments by the new person in the mingled spirit.[90] When Lee specifically describes "killing" the soul, however, it is not only the self that is done away with, but also the faculties of mind, will and emotion. Four aspects of the soul are to be denied:

1. The self (a synonym for "self" is human nature). ". . . the soul is simply the self. The self is the very center of the human being and is the human being, and it is the self which must be crossed out. . . . *To deny the soul means that we turn from ourselves to the spirit.*"[91]

2. The mind (and doctrines, which are of the mind). "One who is in the mind should refuse his intellect in all spiritual things; he should put aside completely such functions as thinking and considering and return to the spirit. . . . When he reads the Bible, prays or speaks about spiritual things, he should refuse his thinking, imagining, theorizing and

investigating...."[92]

3. Morality (an effective willing of behavioral choices based on moral standards). For Lee, morality is neither of the law nor of grace. Indeed, humankind's fall was *into* morality: Adam and Eve ate of the tree of the knowledge of good and evil.[93] "In my Christian dictionary there is not such a word as 'evil,' nor is there such a word as 'good'! From the beginning to the end my Christian dictionary contains only one word—'Christ'! I understand neither good nor evil. I do not want help to do good; I only want Christ!... Trying to do good is a real temptation and a great distraction from experiencing Christ."[94] "Eventually, there is no right or wrong, no yes or no—only Jesus!... There is no law, no teaching, no regulations—only Jesus."[95]

4. Natural emotions, affections, and desires. "Natural affection, natural love, and natural relationships have to be cut off by the cross."[96] "Whatever we can do in a natural way with our natural strength does not count in the eyes of God. We may love our wife naturally, but that love in the eyes of God means nothing. In the heavenly account, it will never give any credit. God wants nothing but Christ Himself."[97]

Releasing. "Releasing" is the positive side of sanctification in Witness Lee's theology. It is not a release of righteousness into a sinful person but a release of life into a dead one. Life can come only from a mingled spirit which has been divided from a subdued soul and body. "Our spirit is the organ to receive God and to contain Him."[98] Lee exhorts Local Church members to disavow the soul (self) and pursue instead the spirit, where the Godhead reigns.[99] Concentration on one's inner life, which is Christ in one's spirit, yields two by-products: it effectively mitigates the soul's influence in the disciple's life, and it releases the Godhead's attributes into the whole person.[100]

The bridge over the ontological schism is the human

heart. The mingled divine-human spirit is ever waiting, but is shackled until the heart (which includes elements of soul and spirit) wants to "touch the Lord."

Although there are some objective helps for a spiritual life—teachers, the Bible, the circumstances of life (hard work, obedience, chastisement, providential problems) and the true church (the Local Church)—the final attainment of true spirituality is mystical. For Witness Lee, spiritual maturity is a movement inward which leaves all outward tests and helps behind. "To determine whether a person has grown in life, we must observe the condition of his enlightenment within."[101] "The condition in the holy of holies typifies the condition in our spirit. When a man turns to his spirit, he enters into the holy of holies. He no longer lives according to the feeling of his soul, nor does he display anything before men. Everything is hidden; it is no longer on the surface, but deep within. At this time, his spiritual life attains the degree of maturity."[102]

Further, because sanctification is progressive, Lee can delineate certain elements of what seems to be a superspirituality. When analyzed, that spirituality is composed of:

increase of the element of God;
increase of the stature of Christ;
expanding of the ground of the Holy Spirit;
decrease of the human element;
breaking of the natural life;
subduing of every part of the soul.[103]

Thus, perpetually higher degrees of possessing God's life are attainable.

The select few who climb the pinnacles of sanctification are the elders of the Local Church. The Old Testament priesthood is the archetype for the Local Church clergy-elders. In practice, these superspiritual people constitute an elite possessing permanent authority under Witness Lee's direction.

Such a group is under the anointing of the Holy Spirit
and has the urim and the thummim. Thus, they can obtain
the judgment, the decision of the Lord. They will be able to
judge and decide any matter that may arise.... [104]

At a certain point, something new must be started
among you. Formerly, all you have enjoyed has been
Christ as the lamb, as the manna, and at the most as the
rock with the living water. Now you must enjoy Christ in a
new way, in a new stage, . . . you must confess that it is
rather difficult to pass this fifth item [the experience of
Christ as the high priest so that we can assume the priest-
hood]. Not many groups of the Lord's children ever realize
the priesthood. [105]

Local Church members must submit to the elders' counsel, if
their own sanctification is to be deemed credible. [106] Submission to the elders entails obedience, a yielding of the prerogative to challenge them—even in situations where they are in
error. [107] The elders are regarded somewhat like the enlightened gurus of Eastern religions. Their superspirituality is altogether subjective. It cannot be measured or expressed in terms commonly associated with righteousness
and piety. By definition the elders are beyond objective judgment. They seem to move as though clothed in beatific robes.
They are awesome. They use their spirits to discern whether
others are stagnating in the body-soul complex. [108] They "release the Spirit." People and evil spirits alike fear them.
Elders are perceived as such only by their superspiritual
coworkers. [109]

A question will no doubt occur to many, however: "Who
could evaluate a person's subjective experiences to sanction
his entrance into that mystical body of elders, since there are
no objective criteria on which to base such a decision?"

Witness Lee has more to say, at least by analogy, about
this magical mystical sanctification. Yet in saying it, he
never draws a distinction between Christ's ultimate fulfill-

ment of redemptive history and how that redemption is applied to Christians.

Biblically, "redemption accomplished" refers to the saving nature of Christ's life, death and resurrection in human
history. "Redemption applied" refers to the work of the Holy
Spirit in bestowing the riches of Christ on the redeemed.
Christ's redemption is a once-for-all, accomplished, historical fact, the merit of which stands apart from our experience of it. For Lee, however, Christ's passion and resurrection are elevated to a higher spiritual plane (Reality)
where redemption is viewed as an *ongoing process* with no
foreseeable cessation. From the point of conversion throughout the sanctification process and into eternity, the passion
and resurrection of Christ continuously descend from that
Reality into one's subjective experience. Consequently, salvation and sanctification do not arise from Christ's historical death and resurrection (which like everything else are
shadows in the temporal world); rather, they stem from the
inward experience of Reality steadily entering the spirit.[110]

According to Lee, believers do not inherit the benefits of
"redemption applied"; they experience the death and resurrection of Christ in the higher spiritual Reality—the continual process of "redemption accomplished."[111] They thus
experience the perpetual death and resurrection of Christ
subjectively and directly rather than vicariously.

Not fully appreciating God's forensic declaration that
Christ's death is substitutionary, Lee asserts the *experience*
of Christ's crucifixion by Local Church members.[112] "Now all
we need is a mass reproduction of this mingling. We all need,
experientially, to have Christ incarnated into us. Then He
must bring us through death and resurrection into God. The
more we pass through the cross and into the resurrection, '
the more we will be in God."[113]

Present-tense salvation and sanctification occur in the
spirit when one mystically experiences what the Lord his-

torically experienced. "To be holy means to have something
of God mingled with us. Holiness is not a matter of action,
but a matter of nature, for holiness is God's nature. It is not
what we do, but how much we have been mingled with
God."[114]

Such salvation and sanctification touch the ordinary
world of soul and body as "anointing" or "feelings" or a
"sense" or "flowing." When one is in the flesh, one senses
death—weakness, emptiness, depression, darkness, restriction and pain. But when one is in the spirit, one senses
life—strength, satisfaction, liveliness, brightness, comfort,
ease—automatically welling up within.[115] Lee recalls that
before his conversion he did not experience a "living feeling"
coursing through his person. As he grew in his love for God,
however, Lee began to sense a "flowing" within himself
which he equates with God's indwelling presence.[116]

With the old self put to death and the Triune God flowing
out of the mingled spirit, God can transform the soul and
mingle with the soul, the self.[117] The body and even one's
conduct are affected. Such a sanctification produces several
character traits distinct from those important to orthodox
Christians through the centuries. For example, decision
making and morality have no regulations except the flow of
the life of Christ from one's own mingled spirit and the
spirits of others, especially the elders, in the Local Church.
For Lee, morality is related to religion, not to true spirituality. "We must not consider, 'Is it good, or is it bad?'
Christians should not live this way! Our only consideration
should be, 'Am I in the spirit or in the soul? Am I doing this
by myself or by the Lord?' When we use the expression 'by
the Lord,' we are not speaking of the Lord objectively but
very subjectively. We are referring to Him as the life-giving
Spirit mingled with our spirit. We must exercise our spirit
at all times and in all places."[118] "Never check the soul or
spirit by the discernment of *good* or *evil*. This kind of check-

ing will only put us in darkness."[119]

A sort of self-centeredness can occur which seems to be a logical conclusion of Lee's epistemological schism. Nothing external, no teaching or counsel, weighs as much as one's own spontaneous intuition of what the Triune God within one is approving. Lee thinks that is what the Bible teaches about the New Covenant: that no one will have to teach his neighbor. The "anointing" is what teaches all.[120] Commenting on the sufficiency of self-determined inner leadings of the Spirit-spirit complex, Lee claims that exhortation from other Christians is superfluous to evaluating one's actions or discerning God's will for one's life.[121]

Since Witness Lee's sensuous theology derives its tenets from subjective experience rather than Scripture, the foundation it relies on is the shifting sand of the human condition. Lee's perception of the indwelling Holy Spirit reveals this. "To cause the Holy Spirit to withdraw by resisting Him is extremely easy, but to ask Him to return is quite difficult. Even if we confess, repent, and thereby obtain the Lord's forgiveness, the Holy Spirit may still not come back immediately."[122]

Techniques. The techniques Witness Lee offers for jumping from the shadowy world to Reality are practiced most effectively by the corporate church. Although other activities include singing and prophesying,[123] the main techniques are "pray-reading" and "calling on the name of the Lord." Except, perhaps, for the church itself, what Lee calls "eating and drinking the Lord" is the primary "means of grace." Pray-reading and calling on the name are to the Local Church what the Communion meal has been for the historical church. (The Local Church does celebrate the Lord's Supper, with real bread and real wine, but strictly as a symbol and not as a means of grace.)[124]

Pray-reading is also the Local Church's substitute for Protestantism's ministry of preaching and teaching. For

Witness Lee, preaching and teaching are only of the soul; pray-reading is far better, being of the spirit. "We really enjoy pray-reading the Word together in the meetings. It is much better than preaching or teaching, because it includes breathing. When we pray-read the Word, we just breathe the Lord Jesus into us. . . . We come together not to receive some teaching, but to be breathed upon by the Lord Jesus—to take in the Lord Jesus by breathing."[125]

Pray-reading is much closer to Catholicism's Eucharist than to Protestantism's preaching. It is eating and drinking, but only mystically (not physically); it is beyond human comprehension and is a union of essence (not of relationship) with God. "Most of us have a mistaken concept concerning God. We consider that He is so high and mighty that we must bow and worship . . . Him. But God wants us to take Him as food. He desires that we partake of Him inwardly more than worship Him outwardly."[126]

Pray-reading is the repetition of Scripture phrases and paraphrases, usually punctuated at short intervals with cries of "O Lord Jesus!" and "Amen!" Here is Witness Lee's example of how to pray-read, using Galatians 2:20: ". . . With your eyes upon the Word and *praying from deeply within* say: 'Praise the Lord, "I am crucified with Christ." Hallelujah! "Crucified with Christ." Amen! "I am." O, Lord, "I am crucified." Praise the Lord! "Crucified with Christ." Amen! "I am crucified with Christ." Hallelujah! Amen! "Nevertheless." Amen. "Nevertheless." Amen. "I live." O, Lord, "I live!" Hallelujah! Amen! "Yet not I but Christ," etc.' "[127]

In this shadowy world, the words of "pray-reading" and "calling on the name of the Lord" become a source of great blessing. They are the true Eucharist, the means of grace. The bread and wine of Communion celebrations only symbolize the nourishment descending from Reality. True nourishment is an increased mingling of the divine and human spirits.[128] Lee believes that pray-reading is un-paralleled in its efficacy to release the spirit. Pray-reading, he insists, keeps people from using their minds; instead it exercises their spirits. The words of the Bible are to be perceived not by the mind but by the spirit, which is strengthened through pray-reading.[129]

"Pray-reading" and "calling on the name of the Lord" seem to have five characteristics:

1. They are mindless, irrational, mystical. "There is no need for us to close our eyes when we pray. It is better for us to close our mind!... There is no need to explain or expound the Word; simply pray *with* the Word. Forget about reading, researching, understanding, and learning the Word. You must pray-read the Word. Then eventually you will *really* understand it. If you will practice this, you will receive something so nourishing and strengthening within which will empower you and give you life all the time."[130]

2. They are vocal and loud. Worshipers must produce vocally in worship, even if they look stupid. If they produce nothing, they are "dead." The dead are quiet and orderly; the alive produce noise.[131] "Finally, whenever you enter the meeting, learn never to be silent. You must oppose yourself; you must stand against your natural disposition."[132]

3. They are repetitious. "We can worship Him simply by praying, 'O Lord, O Lord.' ... From deep within just breathe, 'O Lord,' 'Amen,' 'Hallelujah,' and you will taste the sweetness and reality of Christ Himself."[133]

4. They are to be done continually. "The most important thing for you and me in our daily life is to continually exercise our spirit to touch the Lord. How? Just by this simple way of calling on His name. 'O Lord Jesus, O Lord Jesus, O Lord Jesus!' Say it loudly. Don't say there is no one listening to you—there are many listening; at least the angels and the devils are listening. The more you practice in this way, the more you will be nourished."[134]

5. They are self-gratifying. "Pray-reading" and "calling on the name" are not praise and thanksgiving per se, but are means to the end of increasing the divine within one. They are akin to eating; i.e., they are like the ingestion of God. Consequently, Local Church meetings are not instructional sessions but "feasts."[135] "For at least thirty minutes each day, we must learn not to exercise our mind too much, but simply to exercise our spirit in 'pray-reading.' ... This is a fixed principle. Can anyone be healthy who does not eat daily?"[136]

Ethics: Doing What Comes Spiritually

A sensuous ethic results naturally from a theology embracing sensuous sanctification. Witness Lee's ethic is based on the sensate experience of God rather than on conformity to Scripture. For Lee, holiness is irrelevant to matters of obedience, faith, fruitfulness or moral action. It is a spiritual essence: possessing God's life. "Holiness is not a matter of action, but a matter of nature, for holiness is God's nature. It is not what we do, but how much we have been mingled with God."[137] "It is because behavior and life are things which definitely belong to two different worlds. ... Some believers may be very reverential and devout before God; they dare not be disrespectful or loose in their behavior and action. We cannot say these expressions are not good, but neither are they the growth of life."[138]

According to Lee, a believer may be exemplary in conduct, pious, zealously serving God, abounding in gifts and power, but living an unspiritual, unethical life. "Even if you are scriptural, you are still wrong; if you are fundamental, you are still wrong. It is not a matter of being scriptural or fundamental, but a matter of Christ. ... There is no law, no teaching, no regulations—only Jesus. ... Go to Jesus and ask Him. See what your living Jesus would say."[139]

Lee creates a dichotomy between obedience to Scripture

and sensitivity to the Spirit of Christ that seems to make them mutually exclusive attainments. Spirit-filled believers are to turn to their own spirits—"listen to Jesus" —and obey the intuitions that originate there. Feelings, intuitions and spontaneous sensations are trusted, whereas words or signs (i.e., Scripture) are suspect. Believers are spared havoc by *sensing* formidable events in advance, thus either avoiding them or somehow effecting positive resolutions.

In no case, however, are the guidelines of Scripture to be consulted rather than turning inward. Lee considers the ethical standards found in the Bible as possibly helpful hints, but never definitive guidelines. All that is truly ethical is the life of God manifested in the Spirit-spirit complex. Yet most Christians can see that if sin were divorced from biblical judgments and if holiness were divorced from biblical criteria, it would be possible to "do good" and sin, or "do evil" but not sin. One can conceive of immature believers whose standard of conduct plunges far below the ethical code of the law, but who remain oblivious to the disparity. In Witness Lee's ethical system, sin is truly sin only when the Spirit convicts such a person and then he or she voluntarily disobeys that "leading."

Ultimately, believers are not obligated to obey any ethical standard beyond their ability to *sense* the leading of the Spirit within their own spirit. Consider Lee's description of a new Christian displaying a bad habit: " . . . a brother tells him that this bad habit is not pleasing to the Lord and that he must get rid of it immediately. He replies, 'When I pray, I am not aware that the Lord is displeased.' To prove his point, the brother then explains to him all the biblical truths concerning the matter. Finally, the new convert is convinced and compels himself to obey these truths. . . . This results in failure, because his growth of life is not adequate. . . . Therefore, he continues to live in this bad habit. At this point, his conscience condemns him severely. . . . ”[140]

Commenting on that illustration, Lee says the new convert's guilt (induced by biblical precept) is a "leakage of the conscience." Lee then cautions members not to "impart to others advanced knowledge" [biblical truths] which may cause a leakage of conscience.[141] Later in the discussion on conscience Lee writes that true knowledge of sin committed comes *only* from feelings that exist in the conscience,[142] and does not mention the knowledge of sin gained through biblical precepts. It seems that Lee allows for a scale of sliding morality when he also says that feelings arising from conscience and enlightenment of the Holy Spirit differ in everyone.[143]

Biblically, of course, God manifests perfect holiness because he is self-consistent, not because he obeys an extraneous, higher law. Lee reasons that because Christians, too, are divine, they should not be bound by external moral laws.

In the context of evangelism and discipleship, Lee says that the message believers communicate is inconsequential. Union with God—being "put into" him—is the crucial element. People's beliefs about God seemingly will not influence the degree of their fellowship with him.[144]

Ecclesiology: The House That Lee Built

Although the crux of the Local Church's theology is the mingling of God and humanity, Witness Lee's ecclesiology or doctrine of the church is also momentous (see Glossary). Local Church members claim to be the only true Christians, the true church. Lee justifies the founding of the Local Church by exegeting Old Testament prophecy and New Testament narrative. He devotes his book *Christ and the Church Revealed and Typified in the Psalms* to demonstrating that only the Local Church, not the catholic (universal) Christian faith, is prophesied in many texts. Lee argues that Matthew 18:15-20 is a text alluding to the Local Church, as are all the letters of Paul that are addressed to cities. Throughout his writings Lee exalts the Local Church with such appellations as "God's dwelling," "God's beauty," "the place of God's blessing" and "the dispatcher of true salvation." "Furthermore, the salvation of God's people comes out of the local churches. Psalm 53:6, 'Oh that the salvation of Israel were come out of Zion!' "[145]

At the same time, Lee deprecates "Christianity," using pejorative adjectives like "misled," "poor," "fallen," "lost," "mistaken," "pitiful" and "heathen" to describe religious non-Local Church people. Lee asserts: "Satan will allow people to be saved, as long as they are not built up."[146] "Building up" refers to the formation by Local Church members of the true church in their localities.

The Local Church believes that it is now the exclusive focal point of God's most profound activity. It is the vehicle transmitting the light of Reality to recover and save the world. Christianity's denominationalism is particularly sinful. Lee appears to be convinced that God waited nearly twenty centuries for a group of believers like the Local Church to surface, through whom he could again reveal himself. Clearly, the Local Church has a messianic self-image.

Nature of the Church. To Witness Lee, the church's essence is divinity. It *is* the Body of Christ; it *is* Christ; it *is* the new mode of the Godhead. " . . . The church is one with Christ in life and nature. In other words, according to life and nature, Christ is the church. Christ is not only the Head, but He is also the Body, because the Body's life is Christ and the Body's nature is Christ. The Body is Christ, and Christ is the Body."[147] "Regardless of what teaching or message we use, *as long as people are put into the triune God,* that is quite sufficient."[148]

The Local Church experiences the blessings of God

primarily when it assembles to form the corporate body of
spiritual Christians. As Witness Lee sees it, individuals
yearning to grow in godliness through a private devotional
life seldom achieve deep levels of experience. Christians who
focus on the Bible and the doctrines it contains will not
"hear" from God.

> ... It is impossible for any *individual* to glorify God or
> express Christ in a *full way* if he is not *built up* with other
> Christians.... All of our problems are due to one thing:
> we are too independent and individualistic; we are dis-
> connected and isolated from others. So we are beset with
> failures and weaknesses. Do you have a certain besetting
> sin which you cannot overcome? You will never surmount
> it or overcome it by yourself. You must forget your own
> efforts and pay full attention to being built up with
> others.[149]

Everything else—all of creation, the heavens, humankind
and even the Trinity itself—exists for that corporate body.
The fulfillment of all things is the Local Church.[150]

Church Government. The true church has a proper government, says Lee, yet history has rarely seen it in action;
only the churches of the apostolic age and of the Brethren
type are biblical. In the context of Lee's overall teaching on
church life, the Brethren movement is weightier than the
Reformation, and the Local Church is weightiest of all.

Often, in reading Lee, one might think church government unimportant, since he so consistently derides forms
and organizations, offering in their stead "spontaneous"
organic growth. In practice, however, he establishes an
authoritative eldership of the "spiritually advanced." Lee
counsels his followers not to censure the elders, who are
entrusted with the ministry of God's Spirit,[151] warning
that "... as soon as you criticize him and dispute with
him, his ministry toward you is finished."[152]

Such authoritative leadership exerts great leverage in a

church member's life, generating intense dependency on the leader's approval in both personal matters (home life, vocation and the like) and church affairs. To differ with a leader's counsel puts one in a "soulish" predicament, adrift from the spiritual flow of church life; submission provides security and approval. Paradoxically, Max Rapoport, the former Anaheim church president, reports that he selected elders on the basis of their genuineness, sincerity and espousal of the "party line," rather than any "superspiritual" discernment.

Locality. The Local Church derives its name from its doctrine of "local ground," which states that there must be only one church in each city. According to Lee's interpretation, the New Testament contains no reference to a church whose jurisdiction was smaller than a city. Lee takes that not as a historical happenstance but as a divine principle. Consequently, a Local Church is named after its city: "the Church in Seattle," "the Church in Anaheim" and so forth. Only by obeying "one city, one church" can the church be unified and healthy.[153]

> Do not try to be neutral. Do not try to reconcile the denominations with the local church. You can never reconcile them. Can you reconcile black with white? You can, but it will be grey; it will neither be black nor white.[154]

> The building up of the saints into one corporate expression of Christ is the real testimony. Oh, may we defeat the divisions! The severest test among God's children today is this matter of unity. . . . This is a real test, a real cross, a putting to death, and a burying of one's self.[155]

Exclusiveness. Witness Lee teaches that only those who are "in the spirit, on the ground" are the true church—so the true church is exclusive. It excludes, for example, "religion." Christ opposed the religion of his day, and Witness Lee decries the religion of today (Christianity) as another religion of forms, organizations and words, but not of life.

"What is it to be religious? To be religious is simply to be sound, scriptural, and fundamental, yet without the presence of Christ. If we lack His presence, regardless of how scriptural we are, we are simply religious."[156]

Those who criticize the Local Church often find themselves admonished to heed the advice of Gamaliel: "Let these men alone; you might actually find yourselves to be fighting against God."[157] Application of that Scripture on behalf of Witness Lee's movement is based on his assumption that the Local Church has the same relation to contemporary Christianity that early Christianity had to Judaism, namely, that it supersedes it. That attitude is expressed rather boldly within the confines of the Local Church. Public teaching on the matter has been somewhat more guarded; nevertheless, Lee has committed himself in print on at least several occasions, declaring that Christians of today occupy the spiritual position of Gentiles in New Testament times.

> Ephesians 4:17-18 tells us that we should not walk as the Gentiles walk, because they are alienated from the life of God. . . . "walk not as other Gentiles walk, in the vanity of their mind, having the understanding darkened, being alienated from the life of God through the ignorance that is in them because of the blindness of their heart." The Gentiles were alienated, not from religion, Bible teaching or doctrines, but from the life of God. . . .
>
> I am sorry to say that in today's Christianity, so many genuine Christians have Christ, yet actually, in a sense, they are alienated from the life of God.[158]

In the above instance, Lee attempts to use Scripture as a basis for setting his movement against and above "Christianity." Elsewhere he declares the distinction on his own authority: "We are simply putting off religion, putting off Christianity. In the early days, the church had to put away Judaism. Today we have to put off Christianity."[159]

All Christians not in the Local Church are in captivity, in the wilderness, of Babylon, and without much regard from the Lord.[160] Today's remnant, however, can flee only to the Local Church.[161] Indeed, for Lee, the dry bones of Ezekiel 37 are an "exact portrayal of the present situation in Christianity."[162] Only the dead stay in Christianity; all vitalized Christians will come out of the denominations and into the Local Church. Those dead bones may actually be real Christians, of the body of Christ, but only the vivified in the Local Church have a strong assurance of being the bride of Christ. As dead bones, those in the body of Christ who are scriptural, fundamental and biblical (i.e., "religious") will persecute the true church, Lee predicts.[163]

The Lord's separating work for His Bride today is in the local church. The local church is the ultimate part of this separating work to prepare the Bride.[164]

Some say that the church in Los Angeles is "awful." But it is still not "awful" enough! We need to be more "awful." We want to frighten all of Christianity to such an extent that the whole universe will be shaken.[165]

Is this religion? No. Is this Christianity? No. Is this a kind of new sect? No. Then what is this? It is the church life. Hallelujah![166]

Eschatology: We Win, You Lose

During the intertestamental period (about 200-50 B.C.), a quasi-political force evolved in Palestine under the shadow of foreign domination. That force became the powerful religious bloc that Jesus encountered in Jerusalem, a coalition of Sadducees and Pharisees. The religious fervor of that Sadducee-Pharisee bloc channeled itself into political-theocratic concerns.

Israel, God's chosen nation, had been dominated by Philistine, Assyrian, Egyptian and Mesopotamian powers many times. Because of their unrighteousness and disobedience, Israel suffered the penalty of political oppression under God's sovereign judgment. Yet the political bloc believed Israel was promised that when its twelve tribes were restored to righteousness, the Lord would send the Messiah to establish political sovereignty and true religion.

In an attempt to rectify their tragic history, the Sadducee-Pharisee coalition produced stringent, extrascriptural religious codes to be obeyed. In the process, they created a myopic view of redemptive history and God's grace. They thought that obedience to the new laws would cause the imminent arrival of the Messiah. Israel would finally be pure and worthy of his advent.

Similarly, Witness Lee and the Local Church believe that the Lord's *parousia* (Second Coming) depends on their spiritual performance. Former members say that Local Church sentiment is that Jesus Christ will return during Witness Lee's lifetime and that the Local Church is the paramount reason for his reappearance. The Local Church believes it can hasten the Lord's return by attaining perfected sanctification, by "being built up" in excellence of fellowship.

"The Lord's recovery" is Christ's regaining of actual dominion over the earth. In the present age, the church is God's earthly agent. In fact, it is the church that deals with God's enemy and casts Satan out: "the Church brings in the Kingdom."[167] God's church today is the Local Church. Without it, God cannot recover the earth and Christ cannot return.[168] "One day through the local churches the whole universe will know that God alone is the most high over all the earth."[169]

More particularly, the Lord's recovery depends exclusively upon the "overcomers," those few Christians[170] who are truly spiritual and who compose the true church, for which Christ will return. Although Lee encourages all Local Church members to work hard to merit the Second Coming, he seems to harbor the view that the true believers responsible for Christ's return are notably the select elders of the Local Church. Overcomers participate in the recovery through their ability to "release" the spirit and to conform to the spiritual church. Only those Christians, only the Local Church, are the prepared bride of Christ.

Non-Local Church Christians will play an insignificant role in the apocalyptic last days. "There will be many Christians who will lose the birthright. . . . They have the birth of life, so they are the children of God, but they still need the growth of life, the maturity in life, for them to be the heirs of God. . . . It depends on the transformation [supersanctification]. . . . Through the transforming of our soul, we will have the real growth to enjoy the birthright, the full enjoyment of all that God is and all that He has planned and accomplished."[171]

In Lee's millenarian structure, the Local Church membership will receive God's fullest blessing in the events immediately preceding the advent of the New Jerusalem: the pre-millennium rapture and participation in the marriage supper of the Lamb as Christ's bride. They will rule with the celestial Christ for the duration of the millennium.

Non-Local Church Christians will not recognize the Lord's Second Coming, just as many religious Jews did not recognize his first coming.[172] Such Christians are raptured after the tribulation; not being of the bride, they do not partake of the marriage supper. Rather, they remain on earth with Israel during the millennium under the government of the overcomers. God will reprimand those Christians.[173] "Some may ask, 'Are you saying that the redemption of Christ is not sufficient? Do we need something in addition to the redemption of Christ?' One day we will all be there, and then we will be very clear. But that day may be too late as far as you are concerned. After redemption, we need the work of transformation (Rom. 12:2) and building (Eph. 2:22; 1 Pet. 2:5)."[174]

Former Local Church members in New England testify that an official but still unpublished teaching states that the majority of non-Local Church Christians will be chastened and locked in a dark room during the marriage feast of the Lamb and his bride, which they will watch via closed-circuit telecommunications.

Witness Lee seems to recognize that in some sense God will always be God and not mingled God-man. The fulfillment of all things, however, including the Triune God, is the church, the true church, neither human nor fully divine. "The Lord will then permeate our body and His glory will saturate our whole being. This transfiguration is the ultimate consummation of His mingling with our being to the uttermost."[175] "Then we will be fully mingled with God, and this total mingling is God's habitation. . . . The New Jerusalem is the total mingling of God with man for His habitation."[176]

In Witness Lee's theology, that semi-divine New Jerusalem somehow makes God bigger, since he is enlarged by being mingled with millions of former human beings.[177] "Finally, He causes us to reach that glorious stage of being completely like God! Hallelujah!"[178]

4

An Evaluation of Witness Lee's Writings

How should Christians respond to the teachings of Witness Lee? What evaluation ought to be placed on his movement's doctrines and practices? The Local Church's exclusiveness toward other churches confuses and annoys many people. Some feel challenged to examine themselves in the light of Local Church teaching, yet that teaching is often ambiguous or contradictory. The Local Church's sectarian approach to church life may offer a broad clue that its teachings are at odds with the mainstream of Christian belief. Lee's strong use of Scripture has often led Christians to overlook areas of his work that seem unclear or questionable but not blatantly wrong. Continuing problems between Christian communities and the Local Church, however, suggest a need for a second look.

Plowing through volumes of Witness Lee's material (ten books, plus many booklets and pamphlets), one sees many debatable points. Ambiguities begin to take on a recognizable pattern, assuming proportions that constitute definite aberrations. Few people outside the Local Church are likely to examine that copious literature with care. Christians who glance at Lee's teachings may conclude that he zealously communicates biblical truth, whereas intense scrutiny would reveal some systematic fallacies of his doctrines.

Lee's hyperbolic style has set in motion a movement perpetuated by his charisma and power. He has captured his hearers with pungent expressions and extreme statements. A theology derived from his personal experience has been legislated as the norm for church life. Yet Local Church members do not question Witness Lee's theatrics or the hyperbole of his writings.

Without claiming that all of Witness Lee's teachings are aberrant, we focus in this critique on his teachings that (1) stray from the tenor of Scripture; (2) are continually affirmed throughout Lee's writings rather than representing mere slips of the author's or editor's pen; (3) seem to mislead the Local Church members who zealously adhere to them; and (4) may serve as springboards for a pattern of doctrinal deviation common to several new similar groups such as the ones associated with Gene Edwards.

Without calling Witness Lee's intentions into question, one can think of several factors that may have led him astray. One has to do with what theologians call hermeneutics, or principles of interpretation. Today many theologians are discussing "contextual hermeneutics," particularly relevant to cross-cultural communication of the basic tenets of Christianity by missionaries. Do certain biblical themes elicit different responses in different cultures? If so, to what extent are those varied responses equally valid? Witness Lee is an Asian who relocated to the West at nearly sixty years of age. No doubt certain structural elements in his teaching (e.g., the deification of humanity; introspective meditation) are Eastern cultural emphases that seem out of harmony with a Western view of biblical Christianity. Certain peculiarities in Local Church social practices also seem rooted in Lee's Asian heritage.

A second factor may have to do with the nature, methods of composition and purposes of Witness Lee's publications. We have tried to put Lee's material into systematic order to make it manageable, because the Local Church regards it as an authoritative exposition of its beliefs. Yet most of Lee's books are derived from lectures delivered in Local Church training sessions. In written, edited form, they have the limited character of all devotional literature, biblical commentary, sermons and confessional statements. They were not intended to be theological treatises or essays. Certainly many Christians have published devotional materials with sermon illustrations that seem to contradict their own theological standards.

Finally, Witness Lee's disposition toward writing and his method of teaching contribute to the strangeness of Local Church doctrine. Lee has a penchant for novelty in expounding biblical ideas. He seems to want to distance himself from Christianity in general and from traditional doctrinal positions and modes of expression in particular.[1]

To the extent that any of those factors render the Local Church's teaching unorthodox, they are also detrimental to the Local Church's social relations with neighboring Christian groups.

The authors of *The God-Men* recognize that Witness Lee may disagree with our systematization of his writings. Yet we think that if he were to reshape his oral teaching into systematic form, his own formulation would be congruent with the one we have suggested.

Consider one example of the need for evaluation of Witness Lee's teaching. Evangelical Christianity in Western society has always accepted the doctrine of God's Spirit indwelling believers. Lee, however, constantly attacks all Christians for being "unspiritually guided." Such an attitude steadily erodes the relationship of the Local Church to the larger Christian community. Local Church enthusiasts single out the evangelical community to proselytize. The conclusion evidently drawn by Local Church people is that all forms of Christianity, evangelical included, are irretrievably degenerate; God has abandoned "Christianity" to work elsewhere (i.e., in the Local Church) in a new and distinctive way. "Do not think that the Lord is in the circle of Protestantism. He is outside the door. Judaism is Satanic, Catholicism is demonic, and Protestantism is without Christic. ... There are only two things on the earth: Today's generation and the testimony of Jesus.... What is the testimony of Jesus? It is still the local churches."[2]

We believe that, although Christianity is wrongly understood by Witness Lee, his distinction between the Local Church and Christianity is valid. Our study reveals that Lee's teachings do indeed differ in substantial ways from biblically orthodox Christian doctrine. Lee's writings intimate that we are in a new dispensation and only the Local Church has been sensitive to God's new way of relating to humanity. "We have the deep conviction that the Lord has turned the age from the age of religion, forms, doctrines and teachings, to the age of the Spirit."[3] "The new way of meeting is a way in the Spirit. It is not according to the teachings or doctrines of the Bible (of course, it is not contrary to the clear words of Scripture), but absolutely according to the Spirit. Do not say, We must act in such and such a way according to the Scriptures. In a sense I agree with you, but I tell you, that will kill you. The written code kills."[4]

Lee clearly sees himself as the harbinger of this "new

way" (or dispensation) and, as such, his writings and ministry invite evaluation.

Lee's Basic Misunderstanding

We have shown that in Witness Lee's sensuous theology the core tenets are derived from and focused on a believer's inner subjective experience of God through impulses, intuitions and feelings. Scripture, however, speaks of God as the external, infinite One whose Word is truth; thus it bears an innate value independent of human understanding or assessment of its contents. God's Word provides the platform for addressing human dilemmas and social issues. In contrast, Lee's theology seems myopic in its inability to address concerns beyond an individual's personal experiences. The Local Church not only fails to express social or moral consciousness but explicitly counsels its members to avoid any public awareness. Local Church members are discouraged from contact with the media (newspapers, television, etc.).

Scripture contains both general principles and particular guidelines. They govern Christian behavior on the corporate as well as the individual level. Negating Scripture's significance, Lee's theology requires direct personal involvement in an issue before one is qualified to critique it. If the revelation of God's will in the temporal sphere is restricted solely to an individual's personal affairs, any Christian moral consensus regarding social justice, politics, civil liberties, etc., is obviously eliminated.

Biblical theology generally faces the question of what the Bible says about a given topic at three levels. First, the boundaries of the topic are determined through a process of cross-checking relevant passages. Second, passages are studied which discuss the appropriate personal subjective response to the topic. Third, passages pertinent to the social implications of the topic are studied. Witness Lee's theology is moored in the channels of the second level without investigating the other two aspects. Although Christian in intent, it is truncated and defective in both range and depth.

Witness Lee and his defenders tend to establish a teaching as mysterious and inexplicable, but then proceed to explain it in an unorthodox way. Consider Lee's doctrine of God. All Christians would agree that the Trinity is a great mystery, fully known only to God himself, yet we have received in the Bible a revelation by which we can understand some truth about God's nature. The mainstream of the Christian church through the centuries has held that there is one God in three distinct persons: Father, Son and Holy Spirit. Witness Lee, dissatisfied with historical trinitarian doctrine, repeatedly states ideas that sound both trinitarian and modalistic. He has not produced a balanced, biblically accurate theological teaching about God.

Some of Lee's teaching seems relatively harmless, if puzzling. For example, in commenting on Exodus 3:6, he says: "This passage reveals that God as the God of the patriarchs is threefold. With the God of Abraham the emphasis is on the Father; with the God of Isaac the emphasis is on the Son; and with the God of Jacob the emphasis is on the Spirit."[5] The implications of such a parallel are many but obscure, so one may shrug and go on. But what of the modalistic teaching Lee derives from the Gospel of John? "After death and resurrection He became the Spirit breathed into the disciples (20:22). . . . The Son became the Spirit for us to drink in as the water of life (7:37-39; 4:10, 14). . . . In the heavens, where man cannot see, God is the Father; when He is expressed among men, He is the Son; and when He comes into men, He is the Spirit."[6]

Scripture speaks of an indwelling by the Father, Son and Holy Spirit as three distinct persons, yet the Bible verses Lee has cited above do not support his assertions. Jesus remained himself as he symbolically "breathed the Spirit" on his disciples; he was still there in bodily form with them.

Nor did he give his Spirit before his glorification; the whole point of his upper-room discourse was that he would *send* the Spirit when his own work was done.[7] Although he promised to be present through the Spirit's work, Jesus used a third-person pronoun, rather than a first-person pronoun, to refer to the coming Spirit.

Witness Lee's interpretations of other texts, such as 1 Corinthians 15:45 and 2 Corinthians 3:17-18, similarly go too far for a balanced theology. From Paul's declaration in 1 Corinthians 15:45 that "the last Adam *became* a life-giving spirit," Lee argues that Christ was actually transposed into the Holy Spirit after his resurrection. In the context, Paul was urging faith in Christ's bodily resurrection. He drew an analogy between the human body and a seed, with each sown in weakness (v. 45) but rising to new life continuous with the previous existence but splendidly surpassing it. Paul then compared the heads of two "human races": Adam was the progenitor of a fallen race; Jesus Christ headed God's new creation. If even Adam was a living soul, how much more life ("life-giving spirit") was in Christ! In spite of an obvious connection between Jesus and the Holy Spirit, it is doubtful that Paul had the third person of the Trinity in mind. He was no doubt simply emphasizing the spiritual character of Christ's atonement and resurrection.[8]

At issue in 2 Corinthians 3:17-18 is the close relationship of Christ and the Spirit. In a booklet entitled *The Testimony of Church History Regarding the Mystery of the Triune God,* Bill Freeman of the Local Church cites, among others, John Peter Lange's commentary as evidence in Witness Lee's defense. Nevertheless, Lange's orthodox position warns against explaining away the text: "We find here such an identification of Christ and the Holy Spirit, that the Lord, to whom the heart turns, is in no practical respect different from the Holy Spirit received in conversion.... Christ is virtually the Spirit; ... the Holy Spirit is His Spirit.... But

such a virtual identification of Christ and the Spirit can
have reference only to Christ in His state of exaltation."[9]

Clearly the work of the Spirit communicates to a believer
the experiential reality of Jesus Christ. Yet notice how
carefully Lange spoke of *"virtual* identification," of a difference "in no *practical* respect," of the Spirit as *"His* Spirit"
but not as Christ himself. Those verses in 2 Corinthians,
while vitally uniting the Lord and his Spirit so that "the
Lord is the Spirit," also maintain their distinction as Lord
and "Spirit of the Lord."[10] Local Church apologetics, by appealing to mystery, again go too far. In practice their teaching has emphasized an unorthodox interpretation by at-
tempting to explain mystically what is essentially unexplainable.

As a final comment on the theological inadequacy of Witness Lee's thought, we might consider his sensuous theology
in light of Genesis 3: "And the serpent said to the woman,
'You surely shall not die! For God knows that in the day you
eat from it [the tree of the knowledge of good and evil] your
eyes will be opened, and you will be like God, knowing good
and evil' " (Gen. 3:4-5). In the garden of Eden, Satan began
by challenging and negating three cardinal truths about
God. He denied the reality of the curse of death, the truth-
fulness of God and the lovingkindness of God. Then he introduced a positive element in his deception by making
false but baited promises to Eve. He offered her the promise
of wisdom, the promise of divinity and the promise of power.
Satan thus twisted God's truth, focusing on Eve's understanding and perceptions of God. Did she believe God? No,
she did not. Unbelief gave birth to disobedience.

Any authentic "recovery" (to recover a term of Lee's) must
begin where the loss began—with faith and belief. The pro-
logue to John's Gospel declares, "But as many as received
Him, to them He gave the right to become children of God,
even to those who believe in His name" (Jn. 1:12). At the end

of that Gospel, John said that the real reason he documented the story was "... that you may believe that Jesus is the Christ, the Son of God; and that believing you may have life in His name" (Jn. 20:31).

In the New Testament, faith, obedience and experience of God are intimately related to each other. Faith generally precedes the other two. It is not through our righteous works that a relationship with God is "recovered." It is not through our obedience, but rather through the grace of God, and that by faith. The New Testament is clear about the priority of faith in conversion and Christian sanctification.

Yet the New Testament's witness to the significance of faith is muted by Witness Lee. In his theology, sensation and experience take precedence over faith. The danger of fraudulent theology was expressed by the apostle Paul in Colossians 2:18: "Let no one keep defrauding you of your prize by delighting in self-abasement and the worship of the angels, taking his stand on visions he has seen, inflated without cause by his fleshly [sensuous] mind."

Paul's admonition applies to leaders who claim direct revelation and consequent authority from God. Witness Lee claims to have "received [revelations] of the Lord" (1 Cor. 11: 23) which were neither audible nor visual nor mediated through spiritistic activity. Rather, his more-than-fifty revelations sprang from his own Spirit-spirit complex. Lee assumes apostolic authority to regulate Local Church procedures based on those privately received divine disclosures.[11]

Human Beings in Bits and Pieces

The diagram of Witness Lee's doctrine of humanity (see p. 50) goes beyond the Bible's own revelation of human nature. Lee's doctrine practically binds Local Church adherents to his interpretation of Scripture as the surest route to spirituality. The faculties of the soul (mind, will, emotion) are set over against the spirit (intuition, conscience, fellowship with God) in unceasing struggle. Hence, although the mind, in subordination to the spirit, may theoretically be used to discern truth, its acceptance of any ideas other than Local Church dogma is understood as "soulish" de facto. Such a distinction between soul and spirit in their operation has no biblical warrant.

In fact, Old Testament *nephesh* ("soul") is frequently used in parallel relation to one's body or flesh, but is also closely united with the spirit or heart.[12] To the Hebrew, the soul was a person's *life,* an indistinguishable whole whose various aspects were often spoken of in poetic parallels, but whose wholeness could never be violated. God created man as a "living soul," so constituted that the "life [soul] of the flesh is in the blood,"[13] and is dependent on God for preservation as a living (soulish) being. Even God "has" (is) a soul[14] —that is, he is a living person; human souls are made in his image.

In the New Testament, *psyche* ("soul") is generally used in a similar way. The similarity or equivalence of spirit and soul is emphasized, not their separateness. Mary began her praise poem with a typical Hebrew parallelism; such a parallelism signals a thematic, logical equality between the two phrases: "My soul magnifies the Lord, and my spirit rejoices in God my Savior."[15] Jesus' summary of the law should make one cautious about trying to diagram the parts of human nature, since we are to love God with all our heart, soul, mind and strength.[16] Although each word may be studied for its nuances (as one might also study "body, soul, spirit"), Jesus stressed the individual's wholehearted, unified relation to God—unencumbered by partiality to or deprecation of any of the four aspects listed.

When the Scriptures mention one specific aspect of human personality, the word used often intrinsically includes other dimensions as well. For example, in Acts 27:37, when Luke said "two hundred and seventy-six persons" were on a ship, he used the word *psyche* for "person," obviously not meaning a disembodied "soul." Throughout the New Testament, in fact, the words *soul* and *spirit* are frequently infused with meanings that defy rigid boundaries and classification. Hence one finds scant biblical justification for Lee's notion of a merged Spirit-spirit as the dispenser of God's will to the soul through intuition, feelings, the senses and noncognitive processes. (For a discussion of Hebrews 4:12, see Appendix 2.)

Contrary to Witness Lee's concept of the spirit versus the soul and its faculties, the Bible appeals to believers in Christ to use their minds and wills to fullest capacity. God said to Israel, "Come now, and let us reason together." He challenged Job to "gird up your loins like a man, I will question you, and you shall declare to me." Adam used his mind to name the animals. Rational worship is defined as the offering of our bodies to God according to minds renewed by him.[17] As John Stott states:

> Now redemption carries with it the renewal of the divine image in man, which was distorted by the Fall. This includes the mind. Paul could describe converts from paganism as having "put on the new nature, which is being renewed in knowledge after the image of its creator" and as "being renewed in the spirit of your minds." He could go further. A "spiritual" man, a man indwelt and ruled by the Holy Spirit, has new powers of spiritual discernment. He may even be said to have "the mind of Christ."
>
> This conviction that Christians have new minds enabled Paul to appeal to his readers with confidence: "I speak as to sensible men; judge for yourselves what I say."[18]

Witness Lee's sharp division of the parts of a human individual leads him into serious problems. First, he is forced to speculate on something the Bible never states: that humanity would have needed redemption even if sin never existed, since "soulish" human life would perish apart from an added spiritual union with God's "uncreated life." Such thinking veers toward the old Gnostic concept; the Gnostics held that a kind of deification through secret knowledge was required for human nature to transcend the evils of material existence.

In his interpretation of the Fall, Lee sees sin and Satan as residing in the "flesh" (meaning the physical body). That concept may reinforce the Local Church's view of salvation, but it trivializes the biblical concept of God's adversary.[19] By identifying the locus of sin and evil as the realm of physical existence, Witness Lee blinds himself to the insidious reality of *spiritual* evil (e.g., spiritual pride) and veers further toward Gnostic tendencies (see Appendix 1).

Scripture clearly calls the created world "very good" in God's sight. Though corrupted through the Fall, it is renewed and rendered valuable through Christ's redemption.[20] The material world, fallen as it is, is the object of God's love; it will be purified and reconstituted as the everlasting home of his redeemed people.[21] Human nature, then, in its entirety, is part of a good creation gone bad. Union with God in Christ does not deify us by adding some missing component. It enables us to be what God intended from the beginning: his own image on earth.

Witness Lee also tends to view God's creation of humankind as an ontological necessity, again going beyond the Bible's teaching. In his understanding of the Trinity, Lee stresses the "economy" of God's historical dealings as springing from God's desire to unify humankind with himself. "Thus, the three Persons of the Trinity become the three successive steps in the process of God's economy. Without these three stages, God's essence could never be dispensed into man."[22] Related teachings in Lee's writing lead on toward a distorted view of why God made the world. Did God create the world not only to enrich his creation with his own es-

sence, but also to enrich himself? Lee presents God as needing to absorb humanity into himself through a process of
"mingling."[23] Lee has turned the *how* of God's creating,
preserving and redeeming men and women into his own explanation of *why* redemptive history exists.

In Ephesians 1:3-14, God is praised for our redemption in
such terms as "to the praise of the glory of His grace," "the
riches of His grace" and " . . . having been predestined . . . we
. . . should be to the praise of His glory." Although believers
are "blessed in Christ" and "chosen in him," and God's purpose includes "the summing up of all things in Christ, things
in the heavens and things upon earth," those statements
express the way believers are enabled to glorify God; they
do not define the essence of God's intention.

One Local Church publication is entitled *The Testimony of
Church History Regarding the Mystery of the Mingling of
God with Man.* Surveying Christian doctrine, it cites many
theological writers on the union of divine and human natures in Christ. It also deals with the union of believers with
Christ, for which some writers have employed the term
"mingling." Indeed, some have even called the latter union
"deification." Bill Freeman expects his readers to be patient
with Witness Lee's doctrine, since Lee is dealing with a mystery in the same way others have done.[24] Mysteries do defy
definition, but one should be hesitant about using terminology that has been largely shunned by the church as
heretical. Freeman acknowledges that the term "mingling"
has been a "theological pariah" for centuries.[25] Nevertheless, he affirms as valid the use of a narrow definition of the
term. Freeman does not comment on Witness Lee's use of a
broader definition of the term, denoting an equality or identity with God. Lee's idea of mingling is rooted in his ontological and epistemological schism: humanity as part of a
lower worldly reality can be raised to the higher spiritual
plane only through what amounts to a consubstantial rela-

tion with God.

Witness Lee and his disciples resemble some of the mystical writers of the Eastern churches. They overemphasize one side of the mysterious union of God with his people at the expense of other equally true and important aspects. Western Christianity reacted against the Arian and Eutychian tendency toward Gnostic idealistic philosophy, perhaps overreacting in the process. The problem with the Local Church publication on mingling begins with its emphasis that a mystery (by definition) cannot be exhaustively expressed in rational or conceptual terms. As used by the Local Church, the proposition that "the mystery of union with Christ cannot be pinned down" turns into a polemical tool. It is used to discredit traditional approaches to the mystery, not so much to acknowledge the mystery's unexplainable quality as to explain it in Witness Lee's terms. In the end, one is left with a demystification of the mystery which is at least as rational and conceptual as any other explanation, but thoroughly unorthodox: God mingles himself with humanity, deifying us in the process.

How One Gets to Be Holy

In Scripture, sanctification ("being made Holy") is one aspect of redemption in the life of a Christian. In the traditional model, salvation proceeds through regeneration, faith and repentance, justification, adoption and sanctification, culminating in glorification. The Bible presents sanctification as a work of God in all Christians. It is always associated with a radical shift from one's enslavement to sin to an offering of oneself as an instrument of righteousness.

In Witness Lee's exposition of sanctification, the amoral nature of God's work in Christians is a distinctly unbiblical theme. As noted in the preceding chapter, the Local Church's definition of sanctification isolates it from the moral categories of sinfulness and righteousness by which human thoughts, speech and deeds are evaluated in the Bible. For Lee, sanctification is a greater possession of the essence of God in believers, not an increase in their holiness and imitation of Christ's character.

The Bible overwhelmingly associates sanctification with moral categories. In Romans 6, Christians are said to be united to Jesus Christ in his death and in the power of his resurrection. Christians are dead to the passions of *reigning sin* (vv. 2-6). Although they experience *surviving sin,* the "old man" has been crucified; the body of sin is dead, without dominion. With Christ's death and resurrection credited to their account, Christians undergo sanctification as they actively yield their whole selves to God as instruments of righteousness (vv. 12-14). Paul was clearly encouraging Christians to practice righteous behavior, a moral category, rather than to "experience" a higher degree of God in the self, which is Lee's emphasis.

In 1 John 3, the process of sanctification is similarly defined in the moral categories of sin and righteousness. "Little children, let no one deceive you; the one who practices righteousness is righteous, just as He is righteous; ... No one who is born of God practices sin, because His seed abides in him; and he cannot sin [i.e., does not continue to sin], because he is born of God" (vv. 7, 9). The "new birth" yields the fruit of righteousness, the converse of sin. In describing the mode and result of sanctification, the New Testament depicts a state of righteousness in harmony with biblical principles of ethics. The converse of that state is sin: disobedience to the laws of God. John's assertion that "All unrighteousness is sin. ..." (1 Jn. 5:17) and Paul's conclusion that " ... through the Law comes the knowledge of sin" (Rom. 3:20) show that God's law serves as the standard of righteousness for redeemed and unredeemed humanity alike. Rhetorically, Paul put it this way: "For we maintain that a man is justified by faith apart from works of the Law. ... Do we then nullify the Law through faith? May it never be! On the contrary, we establish the Law" (Rom. 3:28, 31). Paul affirmed the law as the biblical measure of sanctification (and conversely, of sin). Although it is a kind of barometer of sin, the law is not the source of salvation (or condemnation) for Christians.

In the biblical view, there are no gray areas of amoral thoughts or deeds. Witness Lee teaches, however, that one may do wrong without committing sin, or may do good without being godly. His scheme of amoral sanctification demeans the law. He ignores the law in his commentaries, labeling such sections of Scripture as efforts of human invention.[26] Lee's peculiar redefinition process also accounts for his diminished focus on faith, which he rarely addresses. Biblically, faith is intimately associated with such cognitive processes as intellectual understanding (Latin, *notitia*), fidelity in commitment (Latin, *fiducia*) and trust (Latin, *assentia*), rather than the intuitions, feelings and noncognitive processes stressed in the Local Church.

Witness Lee teaches that believers control the work of God in their lives, thus navigating themselves along the rivers of their own sanctification. Paul placed the emphasis elsewhere when he instructed Christians to "work out your salvation with fear and trembling; for it is God who is at work in you, both to will and to work for His good pleasure" (Phil. 2:12-13). God works through Christians, after their initial conversion, so they can "will" and "work" for him. The Holy Spirit's sanctifying processes do not minimize the necessity of our cooperation and work. Rather, he guarantees our efforts and assures us that they are valuable. In Paul's teaching, God clearly initiates and sustains sanctification; Christians "will" and "work" through his strength. Scripture balances the sovereignty of God's work with the value of human cooperation in the sanctification process.

Witness Lee's view, however, is unbalanced. He depicts a

God who is boxed within the human spirit, needing to be released. Lee's God does not and cannot participate in sanctification unless humans take the initiative to manage their spiritual growth. "Killing," "pray-reading," "calling on the name of the Lord" and "releasing" are techniques and methods by which Local Church adherents confine and control the agency of the Holy Spirit, thus determining their sanctification and piloting their spiritual destiny. The biblical theme of God's sovereign freedom to intervene in human history is lost in Lee's writings on the topic of sanctification.

Lee's writings on the Holy Spirit's mode of sanctification go beyond biblical testimony. Lee specifies the process by which the Holy Spirit sanctifies believers. He sees the Holy Spirit as united with the human spirit, comprising a Spirit-spirit complex whose intuitions and sensations are "released" into the soul. A true believer listens to the Spirit-spirit for those intuitions and sensations which are tantamount to divine revelation. "Releasing" of the Spirit subdues the antithetical forces of the soul and body in a gradual process of "killing" their dominion.

John Murray has made the following observations on the biblical doctrine of sanctification:

The mode of the Spirit's operation in sanctification is encompassed with mystery. We do not know the mode of the Spirit's indwelling nor the mode of his efficient working in the hearts and minds and wills of God's people by which they are progressively cleansed from the defilement of sin and more and more transfigured after the image of Christ. While we must not do prejudice to the fact that the Spirit's work in our hearts reflects itself in our awareness and consciousness, while we must not relegate sanctification to the realm of the subconscious and fail to recognize that sanctification draws within its orbit the whole field of conscious activity on our part, yet we must also appreciate

the fact that there is an agency on the part of the Holy
Spirit that far surpasses analysis or introspection on our
part.[27]

In Murray's assessment, Scripture does not specifically identify the locus of the indwelling Holy Spirit in an individual.
Further, the complete activity of the Holy Spirit is beyond
finite human analysis or introspection. Necessarily, then,
any doctrine that confines the Holy Spirit to introspective
intuitions presents a limited, if not deformed, view of sanctification.

A consequence of Lee's view of sanctification is the estab-
lishment of a theologically infallible and authoritative
group of superspiritual elders within the Local Church. Having attained advanced levels of sanctification, the select
body of elders continually perceives God's guidance. Lee
advocates that ordinary Local Church members seek the
elders' counsel. Elders have mastered the techniques of "releasing," "pray-reading," "calling on the name of the Lord"
and "killing." The mark of an elder is not his righteousness,
wisdom, or possession and exercise of spiritual gifts. It is
his possession of a sort of sixth sense, defying definition and
shrouded in mystery. Detecting an elder with one's senses is
identical to sensually discerning God's essence. It is intui-
tive. By affirming that few people attain that stage of spiritual maturity, Lee indirectly inspires members to strive
toward it unceasingly.

In the New Testament, all Christians are regarded as
priests: "But you are a chosen race, a royal priesthood, a
holy nation, a people for God's own possession" (1 Pet. 2:9).
Lee's teaching undermines the New Testament idea that all
believers have equal access to the counsel of God through
prayer and Scripture reading. Moreover, the Local Church
eldership is protected by Lee from internal criticism. Such
an impregnable structure of authority keeps ordinary members from exercising faith on their own and from taking re-

sponsibility for decision making and holy living. In that sense, the Local Church elders administrate the "willing" and "working out" of salvation for their spiritual subordinates.

Lee's view of sanctification epitomizes the sensuous theology he has constructed. He encourages his followers to sense the presence of God, not to trust God in faith; to sense forgiveness of their sins, not to accept it by faith. Faith is too intellectual a process. Lee has described his purchase of a pair of pants by "sensing" the leading of God's Spirit. "You can sense what color pants you should buy ... what color God wants, what color is close to His nature."[28] Yet Lee demeans "Christians" for seeking God's will in "trivial affairs, such as their occupation and marriage," which he believes are "common, insignificant matters"![29]

The Bible—with a Twist

Traditionally, certain general principles are recognized as useful for interpreting historical-narrative passages, discourses and didactic materials in the Bible. Other special principles must be used to interpret passages marked by extensive figures of speech or literary devices such as parables, allegories, Hebrew poetry, typology and prophecy.

With both sets of principles (general and special) the interpreter's goal is to deduce what the author intended to communicate, and what the first readers or hearers understood the words to mean. The general approach is: (1) to take the grammar seriously, assuming the intended meaning for each word; (2) to understand the cultural influences and historical background in which the words were written; and (3) to be aware of other relevant passages of Scripture that influence the meaning. Such biblical scholars as Bernard Ramm, Berkeley Mickelsen and Milton Terry encourage prospective interpreters of Scripture to practice this historical-grammatical method of interpretation.

Each literary device employed by the authors of Scripture has its own special principle of interpretation. Further, the New Testament supplies a number of models for interpreting such literary devices (e.g., Jesus' explanation of the parable of the sower).

Witness Lee's own interpretations of Scripture seem to vary in quality from valid insights to the total repression of an author's intended meaning. His principles allow him rather indiscriminately to attribute typological interpretations to various historical-narrative Old Testament passages, forcing them to prefigure New Testament events, persons or themes. Moreover, he rarely consults other relevant scriptural passages to illuminate a particular text. The result is an anomalous, abridged biblical theology.

Biblical typology is a special form of prophecy. A "type" is a person, event or institution in the Old Testament that foreshadows a person, event or institution in the New Testament. A type referred to in the Old Testament is more completely fulfilled or expressed in its New Testament counterpart, the antitype. Examples identified by New Testament authors include Abraham sacrificing Isaac/God sacrificing Jesus; the sacrifice of animals/the sacrifice of Jesus (the Lamb of God); the limited Old Testament priesthood/the New Testament universal priesthood of believers. Berkeley Mickelsen emphasizes that types/antitypes focus on critical aspects of Christian belief. Because types are prophetic in nature, important doctrine should not be drawn from those that are not specifically associated with New Testament antitypes.[30]

Witness Lee regards the entire Old Testament as a continual series of types on which he bases a high percentage of his teachings. For Lee, the Old Testament has two levels: the shadowy, historical data and the Reality revealed in the type/antitype model. Lee frequently places great significance on a type's initial appearance in the Old Testament as normative for its interpretation, rather than examining its fulfillment in the New Testament antitype.[31] Such teaching admittedly has a certain charm. Its fanciful applications are powerfully graphic, as in *The All-Inclusive Christ,* where Lee calls on the Local Church to experience Christ as mineral life, plant life, animal life, ritual sacrifices, the tabernacle and the ark in ascending categories of spiritual maturity. The dangers of such teaching are many, however, since both teacher and learner may miss the plain meaning of the Bible's words amid the profusion of typology.

In glossing over the plain meaning of Scripture in favor of unveiling a hidden spiritual meaning, Lee often renders the Bible's historical data inconsequential. He consistently uses the special principles appropriate for typology to interpret nonprophetic, historical-narrative passages that are best interpreted according to the general principles of grammar, history and reference to related Scriptures. One encounters an obvious problem in utilizing typology so extensively and without restraint. No authoritative reference point exists for indicating whether the interpretation of the type is correct or incorrect. Witness Lee becomes the sole authority for determining the correct usage of types in the Old Testament. In exegeting the Psalms, Lee feels thoroughly justified in finding there a prophetic type of the Local Church, not of Christianity.

In the long run, if that principle is consistently applied, the Bible loses its character as universal revelation and as the straightforward Word of God to humankind. It becomes instead a veiled and cryptic book of esoteric teachings that must be "decoded" by an authoritative teacher who possesses the key, a secret wisdom not granted to ordinary mortals. In Isaiah, God spoke specifically to that point: "I am the LORD, and there is none else. I have not spoken in secret, In some dark land; . . . I, the LORD, speak righteousness Declaring things that are upright" (Is. 45:18-19).

The danger of such teaching is even greater if the *factual content* of the Bible is handled loosely or inaccurately in an effort to score theological points. For example, in an attempt to prove that God wants his people to take him as their life (Local Church doctrine) rather than to worship him or do good works (traditional doctrine), Lee refers to Genesis 2:

> The first mentioning of anything in the Bible gives the principle of that matter. This is called the principle of first mention. After God created man, what was the first thing God mentioned concerning man? It was not that man should worship Him, love Him, or behave in a certain way before Him. The first thing God did concerning man was to place him before the tree of life. God's intention was that Adam would eat the tree of life, and that he would be careful not to eat the other tree. This is the first mentioning concerning man in the Bible. Therefore, this is the principle. The principle is that God wants man to take Him as his life.[32]

Actually, the first mention of human beings after their creation has nothing to do with the tree of life, but occurs in connection with God's instruction to rule over the earth, to be fruitful and multiply and so forth—that is, "to behave in a certain way." In fact, Genesis 2 never refers to Adam in direct relation to the tree of life at all, much less to say that God placed him before it. It simply mentions the tree as a part of the growth of the whole garden in which Adam and Eve had already been placed.[33] This is not an isolated example. Lee's emphasis on typology overshadows the historical element of biblical revelation, occasionally even falsifying it.

Under the circumstances, it is no wonder that Witness Lee can say, "I find very few who understand the resurrection of Christ."[34] After reading his doctrines of the resurrection, or of other events, we would not expect many Bible teachers to agree with (i.e., "understand") his interpretations of them. Certainly, few would understand the typology of Moses' bronzed serpent the way Lee does: "After man's fall, Satan, with all his related evil powers, was located in man. . . . When Christ became a man, Satan was already located in him. . . . How could a serpent be a type of Christ? Because Christ put upon Himself a man occupied by Satan. . . . Not only was man crucified with Christ, but Satan also was put to death on the cross."[35]

Like other schismatics, Lee often chooses difficult or obscure passages to justify his doctrinal peculiarities. Sometimes he selects the least probable grammar from Greek manuscripts, ignoring relevant illuminative passages. Sometimes he reinterprets relatively clear passages according to what he derives from more ambiguous passages. Such an approach enables Lee to endorse a modalistic view of the Trinity. Choosing to follow the peculiar wording of 2 Corinthians 3:17, Lee states: "The person of the Lord Jesus is the Holy Spirit. The Holy Spirit is just the Lord Himself." Similarly, he picks up on 1 Corinthians 15:45 to substantiate his view: "He himself is the life-giving Spirit."[36] Yet those texts can readily be interpreted in harmony with other biblical passages. That kind of isolation of unusual interpretations from other relevant texts is a pattern in Lee's teaching. By such methods Lee creates novel yet biblically oriented terminologies that are radically different from traditional Christian interpretations.

Because of Witness Lee's charismatic leadership, his followers revere his interpretation of Scripture and regard it as normative. Uncritical acceptance of any interpretive scheme is risky. In the Local Church, pray-reading has become the most spiritual mode of Bible use. Critical examination of church teaching or practice, searching Scripture "to see if these things were so" (Acts 17:11 RSV), is rebuked as soulish rather than spiritual. Integrity is sacrificed for enthusiasm and unity.

Everyone Else Is Out of Step

What shall we say about the Local Church's exclusive attitude toward other churches? We have uncovered some of its doctrinal roots in Witness Lee's teachings about God, about humanity and about the way people come to know God. If our analysis is correct, we should not be surprised to discover that Lee's followers hesitate to fellowship with most Christians. Local Church teachings seem to conflict with orthodox Christianity at several key points.

In his writings, Witness Lee depicts the Local Church as God's chosen vehicle for bringing "this age" to a close; it is the faithful manifestation of Christ's body in a perverse generation. Opposing the sad divisions in Christianity, Lee has ironically been instrumental in forming a new and divisive sectarian denomination. He has cut himself and his churches off from the doctrine and practical life of sincere believers in Christ, holding out for their unity with the Local Church on what he perceives to be biblical principle.

Witness Lee's mentor, Watchman Nee, held views on church geographical locality and denominational affiliation that were definitely segregationist. Those views can be traced to Nee's close association with the Exclusive Brethren and Taylor Brethren groups in China. From such roots have sprung the isolationist policy of the Local Church in America.

A Graphic Review of Critical Issues

	Lee	Bible
Source of Theology	Sensations and impulses within a Spirit-spirit complex	Scripture
Reality	Higher spiritual Reality plus a lower, shadowy reality (i.e., a sacred/secular split)	Spirit world plus the material world, equally real and valuable; hence, no sacred/secular split
Scripture	Not completely inspired; fallible; not authoritative	Inspired, infallible and authoritative
Authority	Invested in Witness Lee as "apostle of this age"	Scripture
God	Antinomy: God is a Trinity and a modalistic Godhead (Father is Son is Holy Spirit)	Trinity: Three coexisting persons = one God
Redeemed Humanity	Mingling: fusion with God in essence and identity	Creator/creature distinction retained
Source of Ethics	Sensations and impulses from the Spirit-spirit complex	Scripture
Eschatology	Millennial purgatory awaits many Christians who are "soulish"	Full attainment of redemption and glorification at Jesus' Second Coming
Church Structure and Growth	One church per town or city	No limiting factors

5

The Local Church in Action

Some Christians are attracted to the Local Church by the zeal and apparent spirituality of its members. Others encounter it primarily through its undisguised abrasive actions toward Christian communities. The Local Church, wherever it exists, seems to follow a similar pattern of antagonism and proselytism. Max Rapoport, who formerly conducted training sessions for Local Church extension programs, testifies that those sessions focused on the theme of "taking the earth." Implicit in that theme was the idea of wooing Christians. Rapoport himself participated in inducing seventy members to leave a California church and join the Local Church. He also trained Local Church members in New Zealand, where conflicts have erupted in many Christian congregations.

The Recruitment Syndrome

Many people who have joined the Local Church have undergone states of thought, feeling, or questioning and circumstances which we label the *recruitment syndrome*. This process helps to explain why many people convert to the Local
Church.

One model for understanding conversion to a religion
which differs from the beliefs of one's own family or social
group has been proposed by sociologists John Lofland and
Rodney Stark.[1] They define conversion as relinquishing
one's previously held world view, perspective or lifestyle for
a radically different one. The Lofland-Stark model of the
conversion process has been utilized by many investigators
of religious movements, sometimes in simplified form.[2]

We will focus on the first four of the original model's seven
features, four preconditions which combine to make an individual a candidate for conversion to a different perspective.
These factors comprise the so-called "recruitment syndrome." The recruitment syndrome indicates a vulnerability to conversion but is not a rigid causal account of the
conversion process. It may not fit every type of conversion—
for example, those that result from graphic, convincing
spiritual experiences, whether divine or demonic. Nevertheless, our version of the Lofland-Stark model accurately describes the circumstances immediately preceding many conversions to the Local Church.

The first factor in the recruitment syndrome is the presence of "enduring, acutely felt tensions." Tension is nervous
strain resulting from a discrepancy between a person's
aspirations and the realities of his or her life circumstances.
The converts (to another religious group) interviewed by
Lofland and Stark experienced tensions from such conflicts
as unrealized desire for wealth, fame or knowledge; frustrated sexual relations; thwarted desire for prominence and
significance; desire to possess the "mind of God" and become

renowned for achieving divine purposes; and a simple absence of peace.[3]

The second factor is the "problem-solving perspective" characteristically used by the convert to resolve tension. In general, problems can be solved or addressed religiously, by seeking God's counsel; politically, by altering the opinions of the surrounding population; or psychologically, by moving from a distressing situation to a more secure, gratifying state.[4]

The third factor is self-definition as a "seeker." "Seekership" is a period of active search for a new approach, often on a trial-and-error basis, within the general problem-solving perspective to which one is accustomed.[5]

The fourth factor in the recruitment syndrome is a situational one rather than a predisposing one like the first three. It is encountering the new religious group at a "turning point" in the individual's life. That turning point may be a moment of transition, migration, or uncertainty, such as a change (often a failure) in career, school, marital status or living arrangements. The pre-convert, rendered rootless and open to innovation, is at that stage susceptible to a messianic figure or group. A predisposed person at the turning point who "happens" to meet an individual offering guidance into a "new experience" is almost inevitably converted—barring a fumble by the group's representative or leader. Lofland and Stark found that conversions to the particular group they studied were readily achieved by skilled proselyters.[6]

Many people, including Christians, may pass through the predisposing stages of the recruitment syndrome several times during the course of their lives. Adults as well as youth are candidates for conversion when their lives encompass all four factors at once.[7]

In the United States, 75 per cent of the Local Church constituency has been gathered from Christian circles, including teens, collegiates and adults.[8] A common pattern is for Local Church members to be warm, hospitable and engaging in their relationships with others, without revealing their Local Church affiliation. By investing time and energy, Local Church evangelists sometimes gain the confidence of Christian fellowships or entire churches. Then, typically, the Local Church people introduce an issue that causes a schism. The group who are siphoned off into an existing Local Church assembly or to form a new one are usually people characterized by the recruitment syndrome. Conversations and written communications with New Zealand Christians indicate that several churches there have been divided by a series of almost identical Local Church efforts.[9]

A Recent Case History

The following account illustrates the features of the recruitment syndrome. The events, which occurred in California in 1978, were reported to the Spiritual Counterfeits Project by the Christian foster parents in the story:

Nineteen-year-old Rebecca (not her real name) was a likeable girl. Becky had an encouraging spirit and optimistic outlook, although she was not so self-sufficient as her public image conveyed. Behind her façade of wit and vitality was a typical teen-ager. She was considering college, shopping for an identity from the media marketplace, wondering about her future. Becky was also deeply sensitive; she had witnessed the death of her mother and was living at home with an alcoholic father.

The Christian foster parents, a couple in their early thirties who had cared for other children, invited Becky to live in their structured, loving home environment. The arrangement was readily accepted by Becky without objection from her father.

After settling into her new home, Becky had contact with the Local Church. A proselyter for the Local Church, who never identified himself as such became youth director for Becky's small church youth program. Frequenting their favorite hangouts, the young man won the affection of Becky and her friends through his warmth and rapport with high schoolers. Gradually he began to introduce Witness Lee's teachings to the church youth group and invited them to attend meetings of the (unidentified) Local Church fellowship in their area.

Becky had already exhibited the three initial aspects of the recruitment syndrome. The tensions of having to accept and overcome her debilitating background, coupled with the prospect of attending college in the near future, created a testing ground for her faith. As a Christian, Becky was growing through prayer and Bible study. Her life with the caring Christian family was teaching her both love and responsibility. In that atmosphere of trust she was beginning to accept constructive criticism. But to develop stability, confidence and security is a difficult process, often evoking the emotions of love and anxiety simultaneously. Moreover, that process requires time—more than the few months Becky had spent in her new environment.

The Local Church representative's constant concern and affirmation offered Becky immediate, positive emotional feedback. A love built only on good times is apt to be more appealing and enticing to a teen-ager than a love that demands commitment and responsibility. Large group fellowships are generally more exciting than individual Bible study and personal devotion. People experiencing tension and seeking resolution tend to seize immediate results quickly. Becky stretched out her hand to the Local Church which warmly clasped it, tugged gently, then pulled hard.

The youth director looked at problems from a religious perspective. So did Becky. Aware of the tension she was experiencing, he offered prompt, short-term solutions. Becky craved relationships that seemed to afford unbroken unity.

She commented on the absence of disagreement in the Local Church Fellowship. Witness Lee's framework promised an experience of God without having to take responsibility for individual Bible study or prayer. Hours of group "pray-reading" and "calling on the name of the Lord" seemed to alleviate Becky's tensions. Soon she left her foster home to live nearer the meeting hall. Without notifying the foster parents in advance, Local Church men moved her few possessions to a house where other Local Church members lived. The elders assured her that, although the Christian family she had lived with were devout and righteous in their deeds, they weren't spiritual; they didn't possess the life of God.

Forfeiting her full academic opportunities, Becky worked as a waitress so she could pay a rather high rent bill and be free to attend the many weekly group meetings. She abandoned her theatrical interests, and terminated a number of friendships. Several emotional "scenes" seemed almost staged in order to destroy her relationship with her foster parents. They continued to express their love for her, a love that kept expecting responsible action and character from her. Their consistent care appears to have been a thorn which pricked Becky's conscience. Her taste of Local Church life, rather than resolving her tensions, merely assuaged them temporarily.

Becky split from the group after six months. At the time of publication she is still ambivalent toward her unofficial guardians, her former friends and activities, and the Christian faith in which she had once been growing. For the duration of her commitment she never knew that the assembly she had interacted with was the Local Church.

The Local Church recruiter's actions provoked discord in the church youth group. While serving as youth pastor, he had persuaded Becky and two other teens to leave their church to attend Local Church meetings. He had also been tutoring the youths in the teachings of Witness Lee. Consequently, he was called to account for his actions before a group of concerned church members. In reviewing the series of disconcerting events, they concluded that the recruiter had falsified his credentials when he accepted the youth director's position, and so the church relieved him of his duties.

The Response
Angered by the events, the Christian foster parents arranged a meeting between the Local Church man and the church's pastor. Transcripts of that encounter reveal that the recruiter did not consider his actions to be deceitful or sinful. Rather, he confessed the need to possess more of the "life of God," that is, the mingling together of God and man in his spirit. According to Lee's teaching, this mingling is totally unrelated to right or wrong (see pages 70-72).

Later, a high-ranking official at the Anaheim headquarters of the Local Church was personally confronted about these events. He emphatically denied that the Local Church in Anaheim had any responsibility for the activities of other Local Church congregations. Yet Witness Lee's teachings are the basis of all Local Church instruction and they generate momentum for proselyting activities. Further, the Anaheim assembly *has* organized activities for other cities. A large measure of responsibility does rest on the Anaheim church and especially on Witness Lee for the activities of those under his authoritative leadership. When we spoke with Lee in February 1979, we attempted to tell him about this affair but he interrupted us, saying, "That's not true. I know everything that happens in the Local Churches."

The Anaheim official was quick to point out that some non-Local Churches are riddled with improprieties and transgressions. Certainly, other Christian groups have problems with divisiveness among their members, yet biblical discipline is characteristically exercised to encourage such individuals to repent. Within the Local Church, however, sensuous theology does not provide a principled ethic based on Scripture. The Local Church can not be consistent in exercising discipline because it has no propositional foundation to do so. Authority rests in "leadings" of the Spirit-spirit whose impulses may be variously interpreted by each particular "God-man" (see pages 57-67).

Recruitment and Beyond

The recruitment syndrome manifests itself in isolated individuals, but proselyters have the advantage of operating from a broader structural basis. The group of people supporting the proselyter's efforts provide organizational programs which serve as a spiritual shopping mall for potential converts. A group that has had experience attracting individuals in the recruitment syndrome often uses recruitment techniques very effectively to expand its membership. The Spiritual Counterfeits Project has observed the Local Church's recruitment techniques as they characteristically surface on college campuses.

Local Church evangelists project a warm, friendly manner, listen carefully, affirm others enthusiastically and seemingly possess infinite patience. Pre-converts may accept such personal attention as evidence of a true and simple spirituality that allows God to resolve personal tensions, gives purpose for living and produces special servants of God. Usually, pre-converts are invited to dinner at the homes of members, where conversation revolves around the Lord, the glories of being a Christian, and how God is working through a fellowship of believers who "pray-read," "call on the name of the Lord" and feel the presence of God. When an invitation to attend the fellowship meeting is extended, it is generally accepted, partly to repay the time and attention already lavished on the pre-convert.

The unity of thought and harmony of relationship in a Local Church meeting may strike the onlooker as quite impressive. Boisterous pray-reading may recall memories of joyful gospel singing. The heightened emotional pitch and activity of the lively fellowship are pleasantly startling. The people read together, pray together and share their mutual concern for reaching others for Christ, with no variance of opinion or expression of disagreement. Harmony, commitment and God's presence seem to prevail.

Christian sociologist Anthony Campolo of Eastern College in Pennsylvania has observed, as has Harvey Cox (in *Turning East)*, that God seems immediately accessible at such meetings.[10] A newcomer who "experiences God" and also experiences a lessening of tension may begin to invest more time in the fellowship. A criticial point of embryonic commitment is soon reached. Some pre-converts make a total commitment after attending only a few meetings, feeling that "life is becoming a manageable enterprise again." Through Local Church meetings, they sense their spirituality becoming real and tangible, so they begin to participate more thoroughly.

Unlike those who convert, some visitors are uncomfortable during the meetings and do not return after that initial exposure. Such persons often become objects of Local Church harassment. Their sincerity and spirituality may be belittled or aggressively attacked. Follow-up telephone calls, unannounced visits or face-to-face confrontations may occur for weeks after a guest has refused the last invitation.[11]

Local Church conduct at Long Beach City College in California in 1978 is one example of what transpired with different results at Northwestern University (Evanston), Indiana University (Bloomington), the University of Oklahoma (Norman) and other places. At Long Beach City College a number of students were fervent Local Church evangelists. A few students "converted," but a larger number resisted after sampling several Local Church prayer meetings. Those students subsequently found themselves confronted in their dorm rooms, classrooms and campus buildings by the student evangelists, who alternately badgered and cajoled them, sometimes making them late for class or appointments. *Viking,* the student newspaper, investigated the story, reporting that students who no longer wanted to be approached by any Local Church members or attend their events were being harassed. Although the Long Beach Local Church denied any official linkage between themselves and their zealous campus evangelists, *Viking* reporters unveiled evidence that indicated otherwise.

In response to the *Viking* reports, Long Beach City College administrators reviewed the school's policy toward the Local Church organization, known on campus simply as "the Christians," and placed it on probation. The Local Church actions at Long Beach City College are not isolated incidents. Rather, they are illustrative of Local Church interaction at other universities and schools.[12]

Once a person has undergone conversion, the group must employ different mechanisms to engender deeper levels of commitment. In Becky's case, the commitment mechanisms were mismanaged and awkwardly employed. Becky did not experience a transition period between her early days of Local Church involvement—characterized by constant affirmation—and the change to a demanding schedule and the detachment of other members when she "converted." Finding it difficult to adjust to this rapid and radical shift, she defected.

Most Local Church congregations are quite adept at retaining new converts, however. One person who did defect from their ranks credits Local Church people for being the most committed people he has ever encountered. They are willing to pay the price of commitment regardless of the cost.

The Local Church maintains loyalty and affection in newly converted members through a number of social mechanisms which seem to result in a sacrifice of individuality and personal worth, withdrawal from society and exaltation of the group and its charismatic leader. Sociologists have observed that the pattern is strikingly similar in a wide variety of groups.

Loyalty Mechanisms: Phase One

A useful schema for describing loyalty-producing mechanisms divides the process of commitment into two phases, an investment-divestment stage and a burial-resurrection stage.[13] In the first stage, a new lifestyle is created by investing one's time, talents and money in a group while concurrently divesting oneself of one's former fashion of life, friends and interests. The second stage focuses on the psychological dimensions of loyalty, as the individual's goals and identity are immersed in and subsumed by group goals and identity. The stages often overlap, producing a fluid, natural movement to ever-deepening levels of commitment. According to Max Rapoport, who once managed international training sessions for Local Church leaders, the loyalty mechanisms used by most Local Church congregations follow that general pattern. Other ex-Local Church members agree.

Orthodox Christian cooperatives which exercise similarly stringent social patterns traditionally sponsor training sessions in which the rigors of commitment are explained in full, before an initial commitment is made. This practice protects both the initiate and the cooperative. The Local Church, however, does not tutor its potential converts before they make their initial commitments. Rather, the details of discipleship surface gradually and are separated from the joining process.[14]

Investment. The Local Church offers a host of time-consuming activities and relationships for new converts to thrust themselves into. Members generally attend a Tuesday evening prayer meeting and a Friday evening ministry meeting held from 7:00 to 9:30 P.M. On Sundays there is one meeting to observe the "Lord's Table" (Communion) and another for worship and teaching. In most congregations, a morning-watch prayer time begins at 5:30 or 6:00 A.M. each weekday. Rapoport estimates that 30 per cent of all Local Church members attend the morning watches. Members know that they are expected to attend the other meetings as well.

Their attendance at so many meetings accounts for the fact that most Local Church members live within a three-mile radius of their meeting place. Physical migration of an individual to the vicinity of the church leaves many friends and familiar places behind and sets in motion a new pattern of living, regulated by the priority of being available to the Local Church.

Local Church emphasis on attending meetings automatically discourages the development of intimate friendships or creative activities beyond the sphere of Local Church influence. College students have been discouraged from attending extracurricular events except to discuss "spiritual matters." According to Max Rapoport, "Intimate friendship even among Local Church members, and especially with non-Local Church people, is totally frowned upon." Relationships are generally developed only through personal interaction at meetings. During a 1978 conference in Texas, Witness Lee declared friendship to be soulish and unspiritual, confessing that he himself doesn't "have a friend in the world."

Little by little, participation at Local Church meetings adds up to a thorough investment of time and energy.

Divestment. Dedication to Local Church life gradually

leads to giving up one's former life. Divestment can also take the form of drastic renunciation. We have noted, for example, that Local Church policy discourages members from watching television, reading newspapers, going to movie theaters or maintaining cultural interests. If members persist, however, they do not talk about it.[15] Divestment helps a group to maintain a controlled environment where even alert, gregarious members are effectively isolated from the social milieu. Local Church members are often successful business people immersed in their careers but isolated from cultural trends because of Local Church injunctions.

One Local Church mechanism used to generate (and test) loyalty in the divestment stage is "burning." Some time after joining a Local Church, converts may be asked to burn the physical possessions they are particularly fond of or that represent nonessentials. Unnecessary possessions are regarded as impediments to spirituality and any attachment to them as soulish and ungodly: "But God's intention with the seeking saints is to remove all material blessings and all physical enjoyments that they may find everything in God. Nothing in heaven nor on earth can be their enjoyment but God Himself."[16] One night on the shore of Huntington Beach, California, Max Rapoport and fellow Local Church members burned such things as their TV sets, radios, books, favorite clothes, wedding albums, athletic equipment and family photos. Apparently giving these things to the poor or non-member relatives is not in Local Church interests.

Holding the two annual Anaheim conferences during Thanksgiving and Christmas holidays is also part of the divestment mechanism. The scheduling of conferences during major holiday seasons has the effect of separating Local Church people from nostalgic celebrations with friends and relatives. Several thousand people attend annually. No secular or sacred holidays are observed by the Local Church, which also mutes the sentimental associations of anniversaries and birthdays.

Denunciation is a graphic divestment mechanism. For example, when Witness Lee denounced Max Rapoport during three days of public meetings, Lee told the church, and particularly Rapoport's friends and associates, to renounce their ties with the apostate. Rapoport states that the psychological effect of these meetings contributed to the nervous collapse of one of his friends.

The demands of investment and divestment continue throughout one's membership in the Local Church. The original cycle is calculated to produce at least two lasting effects. First, "bridges are burned" behind a new member, making it extremely difficult to extricate oneself from the Local Church. Members who have heavily invested in the Local Church, generally do not maintain previous social patterns. Indeed, on leaving the Local Church many ex-members have experienced emotional difficulties in making a transition to non-Local Church life (see pages 128-29). Moreover, a number of current Local Church members, aware of the bridges they have burned, have told Rapoport they feel trapped in the movement. They feel uncomfortable about returning to a society they had rejected when joining the Local Church. Leaving the group requires strong independent character.

Another lasting effect of the initial investment-divestment cycle is development of a sturdy psychological barrier between Local Church members and non-Local Church Christians. To experience God in an unorthodox way, Local Church members pay a price on both the theological and the physical level. As members invest in Lee's theological treatises, they divest themselves of any other source of spiritual enlightenment. They come to regard themselves as the only spiritual people whom God can use. The Local Church membership is continually exalted by Witness Lee as the sole focus of God's blessing and presence. Christians and Christianity are continually demeaned and derided.

The resulting "we/they" mentality manifests itself in many ways. A clear expression of its negative potential is Lee's book *Christ versus Religion,* a diatribe against Christians. Other expressions of that mind-set are Local Church members' T-shirts proclaiming "God hates Christianity" and their march against a denominational church, chanting, "Burn it, burn it."

Maintaining Loyalty: Phase Two

The second set of loyalty mechanisms in the Local Church aims at repression of the individual and exaltation of the church and Witness Lee. Local Church members whose commitment has lasted more than a year usually enter into the psychological process of "burial-resurrection." To an outside observer, the burial-resurrection cycle seems deleterious to the participants. Participants, however, generally experience the burial-resurrection stage as a natural, even desirable flow of events.

Burial. Witness Lee teaches that the Local Church meeting is the true place of spiritual experience, where God's "best" revelation is channeled. Ex-members testify that failure to attend meetings brought social recrimination or public harangue. Individual experience of God through a personal devotional life is not considered essential to true spirituality. Such de-emphasis on individual devotion eventually deflects believers from their identity as unique, gifted children of God.

Witness Lee teaches that it is sinful and unspiritual to think and act as an individual; the individual must disappear, dying as an entity of inherent value and significance. The apex of spirituality is the active participation of believers in meaningful experiences in large church meetings.

The "burial" of individuality is furthered by the fact that the elders and Witness Lee seem to exercise so much influence on matters of importance concerning individuals.

Many Local Church members, instead of praying, seeking insights from Scripture, soliciting counsel from mature believers and deciding issues for themselves, yield their prerogatives of decision making to Local Church elders. An individual may thus surrender his or her accountability to make responsible decisions in all aspects of life, including occupations, schools, relationships, finances, etc. Sometimes the elders have determined God's will for individuals or whole families without even being consulted for direction.[17]

On Witness Lee's recommendation, families have been transferred to new cities to establish satellite churches. Other families are counseled to join those who have volunteered themselves for such an assignment. Local Church informants testify that the subtle pressures of such "encouragement" are hard to resist. Families have been disrupted and damaged by periodic relocations.[18]

In the Local Church, individuals retain value only as they support group goals and participate in group activities. Witness Lee devotes the final chapters of *The All-Inclusive Christ* to an exposition of true spirituality, the essence of which is subordination of individual goals to group goals. "Without submission there is no army. When we enjoy Christ to such an extent, everyone of us will be submissive to each other. We cannot do otherwise. True love is in submission. When we submit one to another, we are really loving one another. If there is submission among us, the authority of Christ is among us."[19] When evangelical Christians use the term "submission," they generally have in mind the biblical notion of "mutual, self-effacing deference." But Local Church parlance, "submission" means something else: a self-extinguishing repudiation of authentic individuality.

Although submission and burial with Christ are both biblical themes, Witness Lee's use of them is related to Local Church authority rather than to liberation from sin. Concerning the believer's burial, Lee writes: "We have been buried with Christ; we have been finished! Do you realize how big a word 'burial' is? It would be good to write it in large letters and hang it in your bedroom—BURIED! Hang another in your dining room, another in your living room, and another in your kitchen. Everywhere there is a room—buried, buried, buried! I have been buried."[20]

New converts may actually welcome deeper indoctrination that binds them closer to the group and that gradually eliminates from conscious thought any conflicting ties or information.[21] Such submission leads to a unique psychological disposition. Confident that the church is composed of "buried" individuals, Lee admonishes members never to challenge an elder's decision, regardless of its correctness, lest they lose God's blessing in their lives. Members neither challenge that teaching nor confront Lee personally without serious results. Max Rapoport's biblical challenge led to his excommunication.

Former Local Church members report that Lee and Local Church elders occasionally exercise a prerogative to regulate intimacy, discouraging friendships and forbidding dating or confidences between the sexes. Such regulation reached its fullest expression in a northwestern Local Church where marriages were arranged by elders and their wives between people who were only casually acquainted with one another. The regulation of intimacy assures the individual's burial. To relinquish all personal responsibility for one's life, as in the choice of a marriage partner, signals one's total vulnerability as a church member. A submissive church is unlikely to challenge the authority structure, however questionable its decisions or practices might be.

Resurrection. Local Church members regard their "burial" as a desirable state of affairs resulting in special measures of God's protection, care and affection. Sociologist Anthony Campolo sees the end result as the passage from

an individual ego to a group ego.[22] The buried individual is
"raised" anew to a greater form of existence, the group existence. Individuals are raised to a greater consciousness of
group success, Campolo says, thereby adopting a perspective
in which they receive stronger emotional benefits from
group success than from private achievements. The individual ego is subsumed within the larger group personality, embracing its successes and sorrows. Members transcend their individual concerns, becoming thoroughly
identified with church concerns. The member who no longer
wrestles with submitting to authority, but consistently,
willingly exalts group goals, has been "resurrected" to a
transcendent state.

Contented Local Church converts regard their passage
through the investment-divestment and burial-resurrection
stages as an honorable but arduous journey toward glorification. Former members say they seldom felt abused by
Lee but did feel confused about themselves, perceiving their
qualms about the Local Church as temptations to be unspiritual or disloyal.

Authority

Witness Lee's voice of authority carries papal weight. Lee
issues three written messages and one tape-recorded message weekly, distributed by Stream Publications to all Local
Church assemblies for memorization and recitation by the
teaching elders. Departure from Lee's original text would
be severely criticized.[23]

Local Church elders and apologists are quoted as saying
that Witness Lee is the embodiment of God's economy (authority, presence) on the earth today, just as the apostle
Paul was in the life of the early church. Lee does not dis-
courage that type of adulation. He does not dissuade members from confessing him as the oracle of God or the "apostle
of this age."[24]

In *Against the Tide,* a biography of Watchman Nee, Angus I. Kinnear describes Witness Lee's participation in Nee's church in China in 1947. Witness Lee was an "activist" with a "volatile temperament" who was "energetic and authoritarian, thriving on large numbers, and has a flair for organizing people."[25]

Lee, Kinnear says, made certain structural changes in Nee's "Little Flock."

The effect of so much energetic organization however meant that something of the earlier freedom in the Spirit began to be lost. A clock-in system was soon to be introduced at meetings which, together with a full index of believers' addresses, employment, family, etc., meant that your failure of attendance could be quickly followed up. The Lord's Table was "fenced" and you were formally introduced and wore a badge with your name. No longer might you be accepted simply on your own testimony that you were born again and loved the Lord. Witness Lee was careful of course to disown the concept of "organization," explaining that, like a cup containing drinking water, these arrangements were merely the vessels for communicating spiritual things. But he exhorted everyone in the church to be submissive. "Do nothing without first asking," he urged. "Since the Fall man does as he pleases. Here there is order. Here there is authority. The Church is a place of strict discipline."[26]

Today Anaheim church members use the phrase "catching the flow from the throne" to describe their attempts to sense the movement of God's Spirit in their large meetings. The "flow from the throne" clearly refers to Witness Lee's speaking as he teaches during the meetings.[27]

Local Church members have little opportunity to discuss with church leaders any major disagreements or dissatisfactions they may have. In most religious movements some mechanism exists for internal criticisms to be channeled through certain officials, thereby averting open criticism of the charismatic leader or governing body. In the Local Church, however, there is no mechanism to express dissatisfaction, either privately or publicly. To raise questions is negative; to criticize is unspiritual and divisive.[28]

Fear

Periodically, Witness Lee humiliates specific Local Church members by naming them in public meetings as being "out of the flow," which members take to mean under the influence of Satan. Since Lee's dramatic utterances are in effect taken to be the voice of God, such accusations are a powerful blow to the individual, utterly destroying any vestige of self-value. Max Rapoport thinks Lee uses the harangues as object lessons to subdue potential dissonance in the church.

One example of this occurred several years ago, when the president of a Local Church in northern California collapsed under the pressure of public humiliation and was admitted for psychiatric care in a local hospital. Lee had rebuked him for evangelizing "hippies," whom Lee considered repugnant and unworthy of Local Church membership. That man eventually left the church. Generally, however, members who are publicly belittled remain in the church. Lee's teachings contribute to their fear of leaving.

Witness Lee teaches that the Local Church will occupy a privileged place during the millennium, the thousand-year reign of Christ prophesied in the Bible. In contrast, almost all Christians outside the Local Church will remain in darkness and isolation during the millennium, after which they will join God and the Local Church in heaven. But those who are not fully spiritual should dread not only their millennial fate.[29] Lee embellishes his teaching with anecdotes about deserters from the Local Church who have encountered financial and physical crises, even death.

Although victims of Witness Lee's diatribes may be afraid to leave because of spiritual or physical consequences from visits of divine wrath, the prospect of remaining within church ranks is not all that appealing either. Publicly humiliated members endure a phase of being ostracized and alienated from social interaction. Rapoport and others report that being "singled out" has contributed to emotional disturbances among a few Anaheim church members who subsequently required hospitalization. For the majority, however, the public exhortations are viewed as an appropriate way to stimulate a higher degree of spirituality. Lee calls it "the breaking of the outer man." He seems to be masterful at engendering an exalted group spirit while simultaneously making certain individuals extremely uncomfortable.

Finally, Witness Lee's teachings on sanctification may encourage a peculiar mentality of suspicion within the Local Church. According to Lee, a person's spirituality is sensed, "smelled," or intuited. Consequently, Local Church members are encouraged to "sense" each other and outsiders. A person's "vibrations" will indicate that person's level of growth in possession of the life of God. Seeking such ethereal vibrations can produce suspicion. Two members who meet attempt not only to receive spiritual vibrations from the other person, but also to transmit their invisible psyches by giving off spiritual vibrations. Since character assessments are based on the reception of such vibrations, stress is often produced in individuals who are socially handicapped or have difficulty generating a "magnetic" personality. Vibing may also be awkward for non-members when it becomes apparent that a psychic dimension is influencing the encounter.

To conclude, the Spiritual Counterfeits Project believes that those social dynamics are a natural consequence of Witness Lee's sensuous theology. In his theological system there are no intrinsic restraints to prevent their abusive application. His theology strips the Bible of its authority to pinpoint theological or moral abuses and to correct them.

The Aftermath

The defection of Max Rapoport, another high administrator and several elders has created a major crisis for the Local Church. Several hundred established members around the country have recently left the church. More dissenters appear to be "waiting in the wings." Another matter of concern is Witness Lee's age; he is in his midseventies. The apparent cohesiveness of the movement, including members' loyalty to it, some members believe, will break up upon the death of Witness Lee. Obviously they believe Lee himself to be an indispensible part of the unity of the Local Church.

Since the Local Church will continue to be under stress during its period of transition, Christians should cultivate a sympathetic insight into the problems of both its members and its defectors. In particular, sensitivity from the Christian community can facilitate ex-members' wholesome reentry into the mainstream of culture. In her 1979 article in *Psychology Today,* psychologist Margaret Singer describes the problems of many ex-members of new religious movements as they reenter society.[30] A profile of ex-Local Church members' experiences strongly resembles the pattern observed by Singer.

Singer's ex-members tended to slip into depression, loneliness, indecisiveness and blurred mental acuity, and felt the loss of elite status during the first few months after their defection. Formerly, their religious life provided a "24-hour regime of ritual, work, worship, and community.... When members leave, a sense of meaninglessness often reappears."[31] Similarly, according to Max Rapoport, ex-members of the Local Church feel a loss of esteem and purposefulness derived from their former participation in group activities. Private, unorganized, unstructured time tends to produce depression. Feelings of having been exploited or duped and of having wasted valuable time accentuate their despondency. Ex-members "speak of their regret for the lost years during which they wandered off the main paths of everyday life: they regret being out of step and behind their peers in career and life pursuits. They feel a loss of innocence and self-esteem if they come to believe that they were used, or that they wrongly surrendered their autonomy."[32]

Loneliness is also a problem. Leaving the Local Church, one is forced to establish new friendships and social patterns in a world (including Christian churches) one formerly believed to be satanically dominated. That world may be equally cautious about accepting the defectors. Singer describes the "fishbowl" effect: "A special problem . . . is the constant watchfulness of family and friends. . . . Mild dissociation, deep preoccupations, temporary altered states of consciousness," and in fact any positive remarks about their former religious association "can cause alarm in a former member's family."[33] Rapoport says that many Local Church ex-members are establishing good relations with each other, although the psychological aftermath is still debilitating. Many have no warm community to which to retreat. (Becky is an example of a person who is now rootless, her desire for fellowship with other Christians now seems doused by her Local Church experience.) Further, according to Singer, the same tensions and problems that precipitated conversion may reappear in equal force, further complicating the sorting-out process. Ex-members "must also deal with family and personal issues left unresolved at the time of conversion."[34]

Blurred mental acuity is a problem faced by Local Church defectors, Rapoport says, partly because Witness Lee intentionally designs instructions to carry inherent logical difficulties that impede clear understanding. Bafflement results quite naturally from coping with the contradictions and dissonant expressions of Lee's theology. An example of Lee's ability to confuse his audience is an eyewitness account of Lee publicly slamming his Bible to the floor, condemning it as a book of death, then picking it up and cooing that it is a holy book that should be listened to. A constant diet of such contrivances tends to numb a person to the appropriate use and purpose of language in spiritually oriented dialogues. Lee's unusual use of language and his emphasis on the irrational ("get out of your mind and turn to your spirit"), leave a residual effect on many ex-members, who need a period of reorientation.

Singer reports the comment of one ex-member of a particular new religion (not the Local Church): "The group had slowly, a step at a time, cut me off from anything but the simplest right-wrong notions. They keep you from thinking and reasoning about all the contingencies by always telling you, 'Don't doubt, don't be negative.' After a while you hardly think about anything except in yes-no, right-wrong, simple-minded ways."[35] Singer notes that it may take six to eighteen months for defectors to function again at a level commensurate with their histories and talents.[36] That has been true for many Local Church defectors.

A shadow hanging over those who have left the Local Church is their loss of elite status. Some feel they have betrayed God despite their firm intellectual conviction that leaving the Local Church was the right decision. They are burdened with guilt for having aborted the special messianic task that God was performing through them.[37] As an ex-member of another group told Margaret Singer, "they get you to believing that they alone know how to save the world. You think you are in the vanguard of history. . . . You have been called out of the anonymous masses to assist the messiah. . . . They have arrived at the humbling and exalting conclusion that they are more valuable to God, to history, and to the future than other people are." Singer comments, "Clearly one of the more poignant comedowns of postgroup life is the end of feeling a chosen person, a member of an elite."[38]

Some ex-members of the Local Church also suffer weight loss, extreme nervousness and flashbacks to moments of humiliation or distress in church meetings, along with fear of physical reprisal from the Local Church or from God.

As ex-Local Church members begin filtering into other Christian fellowships, one can expect that many will undergo periods of vacillation as they recall positive aspects of Local Church life, such as their old congregation's total commitment and willingness to serve others. Such vacillation is a normal by-product of traumatic emotional upheaval and does not necessarily denote a major relapse or regression. Christians should dialogue with those who have "come out," listening to the positive aspects of their experiences without putting them down. According to Singer, " ... returnees often want to talk to people about positive aspects" of their experience. "Yet they commonly feel that others refuse to hear anything but the negative aspects." If friends and family hope to help, they need to know something about the group's program. "A capacity to explain certain behavioral reconstruction techniques is also important."[39]

Singer makes another comment about those who have been conditioned by their group's condemnation of the beliefs and conduct of outsiders: "Ex-members tend to remain hypercritical of much of the ordinary behavior of humans. This makes re-entry still harder. When parents, friends, or therapists try to convince them to be less rigid in their attitudes, they tend to see such as evidence of casual moral relativism."[40] Local Church people have been isolated from certain cultural stimuli during their active membership. Because their informal conversations have been largely restricted to overtly spiritual, biblical topics, their interests in other issues have understandably atrophied. In general, the Christian community should exercise patience while helping them discover a broader meaning of the lordship of Jesus Christ.

Actually, few Local Church "returnees" will have left the church for doctrinal reasons. Ex-members tend to maintain a strong core of Witness Lee's teachings, which they bring with them to Bible studies and prayer meetings. When Lee's teachings surface in group discussions, they should be discussed openly, not automatically viewed as propaganda intended to convert others. Christians should remember that in an atmosphere of openness to truth, the Holy Spirit has a way of getting through to "make crooked paths straight."

Conclusion

The Local Church is an anomaly within the larger Christian community. With the same voice that it decries Christianity it also proclaims itself as the one true Christian church. How then are we to understand the stance this church takes toward the biblical Christian faith? And where does the Local Church stand in the context of broader cultural concerns?

Currently in America there are a proliferation of cultural forces that are fostering new social structures. Promoters of change stoke their followers with hopes for a new age. Many religious movements, striving to provide values powerful enough to reglue Western civilization, are organizing and erecting social structures which they hope will stabilize society and provide a base for future social vitality.

Other movements, not interested in larger cultural issues, reject involvement with restructuring the culture and prefer to focus on more narrow, individual concerns. In religion, this has generally led to an overarching emphasis on personal piety.

Seen in this context the Local Church responds to changes in Western culture by focusing on a nonorthodox view of sanctification. Local Church social behavior is understood by members as the unmediated experience of God's presence and power.

As we have seen in the analysis in the preceding chapters, however, the Local Church offers a view of sanctification that does injustice to biblical perspectives. Instead of emphasizing the biblical concepts that Christians should be salt and light to surrounding society, the Local Church concentrates on propagating a message of social isolation. Instead of establishing Christian fellowship groups who turn outward in service to the larger human community and who find further fellowship with other Christian communities, Local Church groups turn inward for direction in their lives.

We respect the Local Church's desire to revive the church's love and obedience toward God. Their readiness to suffer misunderstanding, even persecution, is exemplary. Their zeal for witnessing surpasses that of many evangelical churches. Yet churches must be evaluated not merely on the basis of zeal; their faith's content must also be weighed in the light of the Bible and its historical interpretation. That is the only sure foundation for genuine unity in Christ.

The apostle Paul wrote to the Ephesian Gentiles: "For he himself is our peace, who has made the two one, and has destroyed the barrier, the dividing wall of hostility ... in this one body to reconcile both of them to God through the cross, by which he put to death their hostility.... You are no longer foreigners and aliens, but fellow citizens with God's people and members of God's household, built upon the foundation of the apostles and prophets, Christ Jesus himself as the chief cornerstone.[41]

We would leave our readers, then, with three final comments, one directed to leaders of the Local Church, one to members of the church and one to the broader Christian community.

To leaders of the Local Church: If you truly seek unity in Christ, then let us reason together in searching the Scriptures to find the mind of Christ. If you disagree with orthodox Christians on the important issues we have outlined here, we ask you to forthrightly declare your position so we can understand our differences.

We would, however, encourage an internal reform of Local Church teachings and practices that could transform your movement into a healthier, more biblical fellowship. The theological reorientation might begin by restoring a balance of objective and subjective elements to Christian understanding. A more orthodox view of the authority of Scripture could produce renewed emphasis on faith and on God's sovereignty and grace. A more biblical definition of spirituality and sanctification could lead to many changes in the way the Local Church relates to the world. A more realistic view of the history and current status of the rest of Christianity could rescue the Local Church from isolation and antagonism.

We invite you to undertake this task and pledge our prayers and support for all your efforts in this direction.

To Local Church members: For many of you, we have telescoped your years of experience and dedication to Local Church life into a condensed theological and sociological review that may seem unfamiliar or distorted. Nevertheless, we entreat you to weigh our concerns.

As biblical Christians we sympathize with your desire that God's glory be revealed through his people. We believe, however, that God's people abound in a plurality of fellowships and churches, not just the Local Church. We ask you to believe, therefore, that the larger Christian community is available for fellowship, support and help. And we implore you to consider the analysis in this book and to measure it by biblical standards alone.

Finally, if reform such as is suggested by this book is not forthcoming, we believe you should feel free to leave the Local Church and begin to fellowship with Christians whose beliefs and practices more closely accord with biblical teaching.

To the Christian world at large: We believe that the Local Church represents a type of faith which attempts to answer the extreme individualism of our day with extreme authoritarianism, and extreme humanism with extreme spirituality. We therefore recommend that, unless the Local Church institutes extensive reform, Christians not join it.

Second, we recommend that Christian groups and organizations should generally not invite Local Church leaders as speakers, since their extreme views may eventually generate hostility and division in the audience. Nor should Local Church members be granted offices of influence in Christian fellowships or churches.

Finally, we would ask all Christians to accord ex-Local Church members hospitality and a full measure of patience, love and compassion.

Appendix 1
Psychological Dynamic
of the Local Church
by Brooks Alexander

The Local Church uses certain *psycho-spiritual techniques* to guide the experience of its members into a sense of mystical transcendence and collective solidarity. Those techniques are based upon principles of mental manipulation that are as old as humanity, and as contemporary as *est* or Transcendental Meditation. Appearing throughout the non-Christian religions of the world, these techniques, as well as the experiences they produce and the doctrines they typically give rise to, are entirely foreign to biblical Judaism and Christianity.[1]

The Function of Spiritual Technique
Fundamental to many of these techniques is the element of *repetition*. David Haddon discusses this element as it appears in the *mantra*, the repetitious sound of Hindu meditation used by both TM and the Hare Krishna movement:

The purpose of Eastern meditation is to gain experiential knowledge of God. . . . In the varied techniques to this end in the mystical traditions of the East, the common element is the elimination of consciously directed thought so as to alter consciousness. Whether the object of meditation is one's own breathing, the repetitious physical movement of the mudra, the intricate visual symbol of the mandala, the insoluble riddle of a Zen koan, or the repeated sound of the mantra, senses and thought are suspended.

A common example, the mantra, illustrates the function of meditation. In the systems of yoga that use it, the mantra is usually a Sanskrit word or phrase invoking a Hindu deity. The mantra is repeated silently to oneself (or chanted aloud) until awareness of the external world is shut out. The mantra is then continued to eliminate all thought.[2]

The result of such techniques is an often dramatic alteration of consciousness which, so to speak, "turns down the volume" on intellectual activity and outside stimuli. At the same time, it "turns up the volume" on internal effects (emotions, subjective experiences, and nonverbal impressions from deeper levels of the mind). Haddon reveals the actual mechanism by which this psychological result is produced:

> It seems that uniform stimulation of one of the senses is equivalent to no stimulation of the central nervous system and has the effect of shutting down the stimulated sense completely. If, for example, uniform visual stimulation is provided by taping white hemispheres (halves of pingpong balls were used) over both eyes, the visual image quickly disappears and the state of reduced awareness of the external world and increased alpha brain wave production characteristic of meditation occurs.[3] The relation of this experiment to the techniques of meditation is apparent. *The repetitious stimuli of meditation and the uniform stimulation of the experiment cause similar effects. . . . Consciousness of the outside world contracts.*[4]

Spiritual Technique in the Local Church
Consciousness of the outside world also recedes under the impact of the Local Church's repetitive techniques of "pray-reading" and "calling on the name of the Lord." Through this same process, the experience of subjective phenomena is intensified. The *loudness* of vocalization at their meetings (equivalent at times to screaming) also causes a state of hyperventilation, which in turn produces a kind of "oxygen rush" that further intensifies the experience of inner emotionality. The ultimate result is a kind of energetic subjectivity which combines the inwardness of mysticism with the enthusiasm of a pep rally.

One commentator refers to the phrase "O Lord Jesus!" (as used repetitively by the Local Church) in plain and simple terms as "the Local Church's *mantra*."[5] The Local Church, of course, reacts strongly against the application of that word to its practices. Nevertheless, while the term may not be a technically precise description, it seems at least a fair designation, for the parallels between Local Church practice and non-Christian use of the mantra are several and significant.

Mind and Antimind. A woman who lived for a time among members of the Hare Krishna cult made some observations about their use of the mantra which illustrates some of these similarities. She says that once she began the practice of chanting, she "saw that chanting was crucial to the Hare Krishnas' state of mind. For starters, it regularized the breathing, drove out all other thoughts, helped you forget yourself, made you feel a part of the group, and filled up your head: with itself."[6] David Haddon has emphasized that the single most important purpose of a mantra is "the elimination of consciously directed thought." Witness Lee himself insists that this is a vital function of pray-reading, and it is precisely at this point that the unscriptural and sub-Christian character of Local Church practice becomes most clearly visible.

In both the Old and New Testaments the pivot-point of establishing and developing a relationship with God is the element of free choice, based on *knowledge* and *understanding*. Jesus plainly stated that the mind and its functions are basic to the response that God desires from us,[7] and he repeatedly punctuated his discourse with exhortations to *understand*.[8] On occasion Jesus introduced important parts of his teaching by saying, "Listen to me, all of you, and understand!"[9] In evangelism, Paul emphasized the necessity of preaching (with content) and specifically tied his own preaching to the purpose that those who heard it might *understand*.[10] Clearly, the Bible not only respects the mind as an important part of the image of God in which humanity was created, but regards rational thought as a virtual gateway to salvation.

Eastern and occult forms of mysticism, in contrast, regard the mind as a hindrance to salvation and view all forms of mental activity as distractions to be suppressed as soon as possible. The various techniques of meditation (including the use of the mantra) are designed for that purpose. They are appropriately called "techniques" because their results are technological or mechanical in nature, being produced automatically, regardless of the specific intentions or beliefs of the practitioner. Witness Lee's statements reveal that the Local Church's use of "the name of the Lord" stands in that same tradition and is technological and pagan rather than biblical and Christian. "We have seen that to reach the unbelievers, no preaching is necessary. If we help them to say 'O Lord' three times, they will be saved.... All they have to do is to open their mouths and say, 'O Lord, O Lord.' Even if they have no intention of believing, still they will be caught!"[11]

Root of Deviation. The truth of the matter is that much of the motive force of the Local Church movement comes from the powerful inner sensations which such techniques produce. This dynamism is based on the fact that the group provides its members with a collective and vibrant experience of their own subjectivity. The experience of self has been amplified beyond recognition by the alteration of consciousness, and is defined by the group as an experience of "Reality" or "Christ" or the mingled God-self. That same general type of experience lies at the root of most of the occult, mystical and pantheistic religious systems of the world,[12] and we should expect to find that basic parallel reflected in some doctrinal similarities.

Having come to this point, it is easy to see that this perception of reality, in which consciousness of the outside world recedes, is the cornerstone experience on which Witness Lee builds his concepts of the ontological and epistemological schisms. Thus Lee has absolutized an experience of subjective reality. One aspect of such experience is that awareness of objective reality grows dim. Under the circumstances, it is hardly surprising that an interpretation should be offered which explains that effect by relegating the objective world to a status of ultimate inferiority or irrelevance. Whether that inferior condition is described as "shadow" (Local Church doctrine) or outright "unreality" (Eastern-mystical doctrine) seems more a matter of semantics than of substance.

Historical Context of Lee's Teachings

A survey of Christianity's long list of doctrinal deviations helps to place Lee's teachings more firmly in historical context. His basic shadow/reality cleavage is a minor variation of the matter/spirit dichotomy that characterized the heresy of Gnosticism, which flourished in the second and third centuries.

Platonism. One source of Gnosticism was Platonism, which also generated several schools of so-called Christian mysticism. Platonic philosophy was characterized by a kind of dualism which saw "essential reality" opposed to "manifest reality," and "spirit" opposed to "matter." In his *Republic,* Plato presented a detailed exposition of that dualism in his simile of the cave—in which chained prisoners sit with a fire at their backs and, perceiving only the play of their own shadows on the cave wall, mistakenly suppose the shadows themselves to be reality.

The correspondence between Plato's language and Lee's teaching that the objective world is a "shadow" of "Reality" is almost too neat, but if we look at the changes that Platonic thought historically introduced into Christian theology, we can see that the resemblance is more than coincidence.[13] According to one source, Platonically influenced theology faced problems about the relation of reason to revelation and experienced a noticeable tendency toward allegorical interpretations of the Bible.[14] In addition, its strongly otherworldly outlook was combined with a dislike of structured rules of behavior; it stressed the "spirit" rather than the "letter" and attached minimal importance to forms of ecclesiastical organization.

Gnosticism. When we come to Gnosticism, the parallels are more striking yet: "a radically dualistic mood dominates the Gnostic attitude and unites its widely diversified expressions."[15] In Gnostic theology, human beings are composed of three parts: body, soul, spirit. The "outer portions" of body and soul are the province of evil cosmic powers, and an individual is thereby subject to their baleful influence. Enclosed in the soul is the innermost humanness, the *pneuma* ("spirit"), which is a portion of the divine substance, or the ground of reality. "The goal of Gnostic striving is the release of the inner man from the bonds of the world.... "[16] By means of that release, the Gnostic experiences the divinity of his own true inner nature and achieves freedom from all forms of limitation, restriction or regulation.

For the Gnostic, as for the Local Church, the ultimate objective of life is to experience the God-self. That experience (or *gnosis)* is superior to both intellectual knowledge and faith: "He does not believe, for faith is inferior to gnosis."[17]

With the concept of "mind versus experience" we arrive once again at the psychological root of doctrinal deviation. Robert Grant captures the essence of the Gnostic heresy in saying that "the Gnostic approach to life is thus a 'passionate subjectivity' which counts the world well lost for the sake of self-discovery."[18]

Summary

All of the characteristics we have discussed are present in the Local Church in one form or another. At the same time, it is important to point out that there are distinctions as well as parallels; certainly Lee's doctrine is not paganism, Platonism or Gnosticism per se. The purpose of developing these points of similarity is to highlight the fact that the Local Church's cornerstone experience, which depreciates the value and significance of objective, created reality, sets the movement's meta-physical compass in a particular direction which, *to the extent that it is followed consistently,* tends inexorably to produce doctrines of a definite, predictable sort.

Appendix 2
Difficult Scripture Passages

The "nature of human nature" is a traditional topic of controversy in Christian theology. When the subject is referred to by theologians under its technical title of "anthropology," most of their discussions focus around two major positions or schools of thought. Some theologians postulate a *trichotomous* view of human nature: a three-part division of persons into body, soul and spirit. Other biblical scholars opt for a *dichotomous* view: a two-part division of persons into body and spirit. Although Bible interpreters are disagreed as to the exact scriptural position, few have confined the Holy Spirit to a particular part of human nature, as Witness Lee has done. Fewer still have set the components of human personality in opposition to each other, as Lee has done. Where Scripture does pit the "spirit" against the "flesh," the flesh refers to the human affection or predisposition toward sin, rather than to the physical body.[1]

Witness Lee primarily uses two verses to defend his position:

1. "Now may the God of peace Himself sanctify you entirely; and may your spirit and soul and body be preserved complete, without blame at the coming of our Lord Jesus Christ" (1 Thess. 5:23). Lee interprets this verse as describing a progressive sanctification that begins with the spirit and ends with the body. Traditional exegesis of this passage, however,

understands simply that the apostle Paul was asserting his desire to see the "entire" person sanctified, after which he enumerated the components of that person, namely spirit, soul and body.[2] Paul's analysis of human personality in those terms does not validate the concept of progressive sanctification, as Lee insists.

2. "For the word of God is living and active and sharper than any two-edged sword, and piercing as far as the division of soul and spirit, of both joints and marrow, and able to judge the thoughts and intentions of the heart" (Heb. 4:12). In this passage, Lee takes the illustration of a sword dividing the soul from the spirit as an indication that a separation exists between the two. In context, however, the emphasis of the verse is on the surgical precision of the Word of God, separating those things which are integrally knit together, such as thoughts and intentions, bone and marrow, and soul and spirit.

Glossary

Arius, Arianism. Arius was an Alexandrian church leader of the fourth century. He argued that Christ the Son is secondary in nature to God the Father and maintained that Christ is not eternal but had a beginning in time. He viewed Christ as an intermediate agent (or "emanation") of God—an expression of God's intention to bring spiritual renewal to the fallen world. Christ is a god, but not equal with God. The Arians seem to have misread New Testament references to Christ's self-emptying humiliation in coming among humanity, missing the impact of both his deity and his true humanness. The Council of Nicaea (A.D. 325) condemned Arius's teaching as heretical.

Ecclesiology. The doctrine of the nature and purpose of the church.

Economy. Traditionally, the economy of God is not a phrase which describes the relationship the Trinity sustains within the Godhead. Rather it delineates the relationship the Trinity sustains to created order and humanity. Witness Lee, however, distorts this definition to encompass mingling, "with the intention of stressing the focal point of God's divine enterprise, which is to distribute, or dispense, Himself into man" (Lee, *The Economy of God*, p. 5).

Epistemology. The study or philosophy of knowing; the theory of *how* we know *what* we know.

Eschatology. The doctrine of "the last things" (the Second Coming of Christ, the "new age," etc.).

Eutyches, Eutychianism. Eutyches was an official in a Constantinople monastery in the fifth century A.D. He taught a doctrine of Christ which confused the divine and human natures of our Lord. In his efforts to defend the deity of Christ, Eutyches in effect denied Christ's real humanity, making a sensible doctrine of atonement impossible. The Council of Chalcedon (A.D. 451) denounced his teaching as heretical.

Gnosticism. A multiform Christian heresy which appeared during the early centuries of the church. It borrowed from many sources and taught that experiential knowledge of reality *(gnosis)* can be obtained only through spiritual initiation. According to the Gnostics, most people are in the dark about life's true meaning, and only those who learn the "advanced" or secret teachings of a select, enlightened group will know the truth of things. The several distinct schools of Gnostic thought shared the conviction that matter is evil and spirit is good. To achieve the good life, therefore, one must become spiritual and transcend the material world by increasing in other worldly knowledge. God communicated that knowledge, they believed, by sending out "emanations" of himself from the realm of pure spirit into the realm of impure matter. Since each successive emanation was less godly and more material, Gnostics could see Jesus as sent from God but tainted by material evil. That idea was probably the apostle Paul's target in Colossians when he said, "In him [Jesus] dwells all the fullness of the Godhead bodily" (Col. 2:9; see also 1:19).

Modalism. A theory of the nature of God which was apparently intended to safeguard respect for God's unity. It grew out of the early church's struggle to relate God, Jesus and the Holy Spirit in a way that was true to Scripture. Modalism taught that the one true God has made himself known in this world in three ways (or "modes"), first as Father (Creator), then as Son (Redeemer), and finally as Spirit (Sanctifier). The three manifestations of God are three modes or functions of the one God, not three persons of the Trinity as in orthodox theology. It is difficult to harmonize modalism with the New Testament's evidence of Father, Son and Spirit functioning simultaneously and separately, yet in full agreement as partners and equally God in character.

Ontology. The study or philosophy of being; the theory of what *is* and how it is so.

Orthodoxy. A term meaning soundness or correctness in belief or doctrine. It is used to refer to the historic Christian faith as formulated in the early ecumenical creeds and confessions.

Orthopraxis. A term meaning soundness or correctness in behavior. As commonly used, it combines the meaning of orthodoxy and praxis (active practice as opposed to theory). It emphasizes, therefore, a combination of right (i.e., scriptural) belief and right behavior.

Plato, Platonism. The Greek philosopher Plato taught that there is one supreme good in life which is the source of all particular embodiments of good. People in this world cannot know the supreme *idea*, which is the *true* good, but can experience only shadows of it. He illustrated that concept with the story of a man in a cave, watching shadows on the wall. The shadows represented the true knowledge but were far inferior to it. We are all trapped in a cave in this material world, he maintained, and the real world is one of spirit, which our individual spirits know only in a shadowy way.

Notes

The books and booklets by Witness Lee cited in tne text are all distributed by The Stream Publishers, Los Angeles and Anaheim.

Epigraph

[1]Witness Lee, *How to Meet* (Taiwan: The Gospel Book Room, 1970), p. 66.

1. The Local Church: An Enquiry

[1]John Stott, *The Epistles of John* (Grand Rapids: Eerdmans, 1964), pp. 78-118.

[2]Ibid.

[3]Jn. 2:13-17; 1 Pet. 2:4-6; Eph. 2:19-22; 5:25-27.

[4]Rom. 10:2 RSV; 2 Tim. 3:5 RSV.

[5]Witness Lee, *The Practical Expression of the Church* (1970), p. 83.

[6]Lee, *The Economy of God* (1968), p. 23.

[7]Jack Sparks, *The Mindbenders: A Look at Current Cults* (Nashville: Thomas Nelson, 1977), p. 224.

[8]Gene Ford, *A Reply to the Tract against Witness Lee and the Local Church* (Anaheim: Living Stream Ministry, 1976)

[9]Tit. 1:9.

[10]Lee, *Christ and the Church Revealed and Typified in the Psalms* (1972), p. 199.

[11]Jn. 8:31-32.

2. History of the Movement: A Short Overview

[1]Leslie Lyall, *Three of China's Mighty Men* (London: Overseas Missionary Fellowship, 1973), pp. 64-65.

[2]Some of Lee's later deviations seem to have grown out of a misapplication of Plymouth Brethren-style dispensationalism—e.g., his view of the Local Church as the new and final dispensation or stage of God's plan in history.

[3]Lee, *The Knowledge of Life* (1973), pp. 184-86.

[4]Lee, *The Vision of God's Building* (1972), p. 129.

[5]Lee, *The All-Inclusive Christ* (1969), pp. 28-31, 112.

[6]Lyall, *Three of China's Mighty Men*, p. 86.

[7]Ibid., p. 45.

[8]Estimate given by Max Rapoport in February 1979.

[9]Lee, *Practical Expression of the Church*, p. 184.

3. Local Church Doctrine

[1]Lee, *The Experience of Life* (1973), p. 147.

[2]Lee, *Christ and the Church Revealed*, pp. 7-15.

[3]Bernard Ramm, *Protestant Biblical Interpretation* (Grand Rapids: Baker Book House, 1970), pp. 138-42.

[4]Milton Terry, *Biblical Hermeneutics* (Grand Rapids: Zondervan, 1974), pp. 180-91.

[5]Berkeley Mickelsen, *Interpreting the Bible* (Grand Rapids: Eerdmans, 1963), pp. 99-113.

[6]Os Guinness, "Mechanists and Mystics," *Radix*, Nov. 1975, p. 3.

[7]Statement by Ron Kangas in November 1978.

[8]Lee, *The Economy of God*, p. 196.

[9]Lee, *The Knowledge of Life*, pp. 79-80.

[10]Ibid., p. 146.

[11]Fred Wagner, "A Theological and Historical Assessment of the Jesus People Phenomenon," Diss. Fuller Theological Seminary 1971, pp. 188-89.

[12]Lee, *The Vision of God's Building*, p. 109.

[13]E.g., in *Christ versus Religion* (1971), p. 177, Lee construes the conjunctive *and* to mean union of essence rather than compounding of substantives. Generally when we say, "Dick and Sally run," we do not mean that Dick and Sally have become one. Instead, Dick and Sally are still two entities performing the same kind of action.

[14]Lee, *The Knowledge of Life*, pp. 215-16.

[15]Lee, *How to Meet*, p. 97.

[16]Ibid., p. 94.

[17]Lee, *The Knowledge of Life*, p. 146.

[18]Lee, *A Time with the Lord* (no date), p. 8.

[19]Lee, *Christ versus Religion*, pp. 152-53.

[20]Lee, *Christ and the Church Revealed*, p. 40.

[21]Lee, *Pray-Reading the Word* (no date), pp. 6-7.

[22]Lee, *Christ versus Religion,* pp. 9-10.

[23]Ibid., p. 53.

[24]Ibid., p. 95.

[25]Ibid., p. 152.

[26]Lee, *Christ and the Church Revealed,* pp. 128-29.

[27]E.g., Bible history demonstrates spiritual principles (Lee, *How to Meet,* p. 27); the first mention of anything gives the foremost use of it (ibid., p. 30); man's words speak of the law, while God's words speak of grace (Lee, *Christ and the Church Revealed,* pp. 9-10).

[28]E.g., interpretations of Mt. 28:1, 10 in Lee, *Christ versus Religion,* pp. 84, 87.

[29]Lee, *The Knowledge of Life,* pp. 202-4; Lee, *Christ versus Religion,* pp. 101, 106.

[30]Lee, *Christ versus Religion,* p. 107.

[31]Ibid., p. 102.

[32]Lee, *Concerning the Triune God–the Father, the Son, and the Spirit* (no date), p. 23.

[33]Lee, *The All-Inclusive Christ,* p. 20.

[34]Lee, *Christ and the Church Revealed,* p. 112.

[35]Lee, *The Practical Expression of the Church,* p. 161.

[36]Lee, *How to Meet,* p. 44.

[37]Witness Lee et al., *False Accusations Exposed and Refuted in the Light of the Scriptures* (Anaheim, Calif.: Living Stream Ministry, no date), p. 2; Lee, *What a Heresy–Two Divine Fathers, Two Life-Giving Spirits, and Three Gods!* (1977), pp. 3-5.

[38]Lee, *The Clear Scriptural Revelation Concerning the Triune God* (no date); *Concerning the Triune God–the Father, the Son, and the Spirit; The Economy of God,* pp. 10, 46; *The Knowledge of Life,* p. 40; *The Practical Expression of the Church,* pp. 8, 43; *What a Heresy.*

[39]Lee, *Concerning the Triune God,* p. 31.

[40]Lee, *The Economy of God,* p. 10.

[41]Ibid., p. 37.

[42]Lee, *The Experience of Life,* pp. 181-82.

[43]Lee, *The Knowledge of Life,* p. 33.

[44]Lee, *The Practical Expression of the Church,* p. 8.

[45]Lee, *The Experience of Life,* preface.

[46]Lee, *God's Purpose for the Church* (1978), p. 9.

[47]Lee, *The Economy of God,* pp. 52-61; he uses 1 Thess. 5:23 and Heb. 4:12, as well as Lk. 1:46-47 and Phil. 1:27.

[48]Lee, *The Knowledge of Life,* p. 37.

[49]Ibid., pp. 24-25.

[50]Lee, *The Economy of God,* p. 106.

[51]Ibid., pp. 108-9.

[52]Lee, *The Experience of Life,* pp. 287-88; *The Knowledge of Life,* pp. 26,

36-37, 109; *The Parts of Man* (1969), p. 42.

[53]Lee, *The Clear Scriptural Revelation Concerning the Triune God*, pp. 3-4.

[54]Bill Freeman, *The Testimony of Church History Regarding the Mystery of the Mingling of God with Man* (Anaheim: Stream Publishers, 1977). This booklet traces the history of the use and misuse of the term "mingling" on pp. 14-21. Our conclusion obviously differs from Freeman's as to the term's appropriateness. In *The Nicene and Post-Nicene Fathers*, Second Series, Vol. VII (New York: Christian Literature Company, 1894), p. 210, Philip Schaff and Henry Wace state: *"Anakrasis*, lit., 'was blended'—cf. *Orat. 38:13*. This and similar terms... were laid aside by later Fathers, in consequence of their having been perverted in favor of the Eutychian heresy."

[55]Louis Berkhof, *Systematic Theology* (Grand Rapids: Eerdmans, 1939), p. 323.

[56]Lee, *The Four Major Steps of Christ* (1969), pp. 6-7.

[57]Ibid., pp. 13-17.

[58]Ibid., pp. 19-20; *The Economy of God*, pp. 110-11.

[59]Lee, *The Economy of God*, p. 127.

[60]Lee, *The Glorious Church* (Hong Kong: Gospel Book Room, 1953), pp. 35-42.

[61]Lee, *The Four Major Steps of Christ*, p. 16.

[62]Ibid., p. 25.

[63]Lee, *Christ versus Religion*, p. 26.

[64]Lee, *How to Meet*, p. 78; cf. 2 Corinthians 3:15-17: "But to this day whenever Moses is read, a veil lies over their heart; But whenever a man turns to the Lord, the veil is taken away. [Cf. Ex. 34:34.] Now the Lord is the Spirit; and where the Spirit of the Lord is, *there* is liberty." The Lord spoken of by Paul is the Lord God who met Moses in the tabernacle, not Jesus. Jesus affirms that God is Spirit in John 4:24.

[65]Lee, *The Vision of God's Building*, p. 96.

[66]Lee, *The All-Inclusive Spirit of Christ* (1969), p. 17.

[67]Lee, *Concerning the Triune God–The Father, the Son, and the Spirit*, p. 33.

[68]Lee, *The Practical Expression of the Church*, p. 43.

[69]Louis Moore, " 'The Church in Houston' Denies That It Is a Cult," *Houston Chronicle*, 30 April 1977; Moore reported a statement made by elders of the Local Church congregation in Houston. Cf. Lee, *What a Heresy*, p. 1.

[70]Lee, *The Practical Expression of the Church*, p. 8.

[71]Sparks, *The Mindbenders*, p. 246; cf. Lee, *What a Heresy*, p. 27.

[72]Lee, *The Four Major Steps of Christ*, p. 7.

[73]Lee, *The Knowledge of Life*, p. 25.

[74]Lee, *The Economy of God*, pp. 9, 26-34. Here he uses Jn. 3:6, 4:24;

Rom. 8:9-10, 16; and 2 Tim. 4:22.
[75]Lee, *The Four Major Steps of Christ*, p. 6.
[76]Lee, *The Economy of God*, p. 11.
[77]Lee, *How to Meet*, p. 226.
[78]Lee, *The Practical Expression of the Church*, p. 43.
[79]Lee, *Christ versus Religion*, p. 87.
[80]Lee, *The All-Inclusive Christ*, p. 189.
[81]Lee, *The Economy of God*, p. 27.
[82]Ibid., p. 9.
[83]Lee, *The Knowledge of Life*, p. 31.
[84]Ibid., p. 85.
[85]Lee, *The Economy of God*, pp. 168-69.
[86]Lee, *The Practical Expression of the Church*, p. 15.
[87]Lee, *The Knowledge of Life*, pp. 79-80, 182-92.
[88]Lee, *The All-Inclusive Spirit of Christ*, p. 24.
[89]Lee, *The Knowledge of Life*, pp. 73-74.
[90]Lee, *The Parts of Man*, pp. 30-32, 44.
[91]Lee, *The Economy of God*, p. 100.
[92]Lee, *The Knowledge of Life*, p. 83.
[93]Ibid., pp. 173-74.
[94]Lee, *The Economy of God*, p. 38.
[95]Lee, *Christ versus Religion*, pp. 63-64.
[96]Lee, *The Economy of God*, p. 119.
[97]*The Stream*, 15, No. 1 (February 1977), p. 20.
[98]Lee, *The Economy of God*, p. 37.
[99]Ibid., p. 33.
[100]Ibid., p. 102.
[101]Lee, *The Knowledge of Life*, p. 201.
[102]Lee, *The Experience of Life*, p. 259.
[103]See Lee, *The Knowledge of Life*, pp. 177-80.
[104]Lee, *The All-Inclusive Christ*, p. 122.
[105]Ibid., p. 133.
[106]Ibid., p. 146.
[107]Ibid., pp. 151-52.
[108]Lee, *The Experience of Life*, p. 332.
[109]Ibid., p. 345.
[110]Lee, *How to Meet*, p. 212.
[111]Lee, *The Knowledge of Life*, p. 129.
[112]Lee, *The Economy of God*, p. 127.
[113]Lee, *The Vision of God's Building*, p. 192.
[114]Ibid., p. 208.
[115]Lee, *The Knowledge of Life*, pp. 45-49.
[116]Lee, *The Economy of God*, pp. 146-47.
[117]Ibid., p. 115.
[118]Lee, *The Key to Experiencing Christ–the Human Spirit* (no date), p. 12.

[119]Lee, *The Economy of God*, p. 121.

[120]Lee, *The Knowledge of Life*, pp. 34, 160, 164; Heb. 8:10-11; 1 Jn. 2:27.

[121]Lee, *The Knowledge of Life*, p. 66.

[122]Ibid., p. 214.

[123]Lee, *How to Meet*, pp. 84-85.

[124]This statement was made in interviews with several former Local Church members.

[125]Lee, *How to Meet*, p. 42.

[126]Lee, *The Vision of God's Building*, p. 73.

[127]Lee, *Pray-Reading the Word*, pp. 8-9.

[128]Ibid., pp. 1-4.

[129]Lee, *The Practical Expression of the Church*, pp. 144-45.

[130]Lee, *Pray-Reading the Word*, pp. 8-10.

[131]Lee, *Christ versus Religion*, pp. 30-31, 43-44; *How to Meet*, pp. 117-18, 214, 219.

[132]Lee, *How to Meet*, p. 114.

[133]Lee, *A Simple Way to Touch the Lord*, pp. 8-10.

[134]Lee, *How to Meet*, p. 111.

[135]Lee, *Christ versus Religion*, p. 15.

[136]Lee, *A Time with the Lord* (no date), p. 3.

[137]Lee, *The Vision of God's Building*, p. 208.

[138]Lee, *The Knowledge of Life*, p. 174.

[139]Lee, *Christ versus Religion*, pp. 63-64.

[140]Lee, *The Experience of Life*, p. 112.

[141]Ibid., p. 113.

[142]Ibid., p. 121.

[143]Ibid., p. 115.

[144]Lee, *Christ versus Religion*, p. 89.

[145]Lee, *Christ and the Church Revealed*, p. 95.

[146]Lee, *God's Purpose For the Church* (1978), p. 10. "The Lord is recovering something on this earth which is absolutely different from Christianity and any religion" *(How to Meet,* p. 66).

[147]Lee, *The Practical Expression of the Church*, p. 14.

[148]Lee, *Christ versus Religion*, p. 89. Italics added.

[149]Lee, *The Vision of God's Building*, p. 15.

[150]Lee, *The Practical Expression of the Church*, pp. 7-10.

[151]Lee, *The Knowledge of Life*, p. 215.

[152]Ibid.

[153]Lee, *The Practical Expression of the Church*, pp. 57-58, 68-71, 107; *The All-Inclusive Christ*, pp. 136, 179.

[154]Lee, *The Practical Expression of the Church*, p. 92.

[155]Lee, *The Vision of God's Building*, p. 19.

[156]Lee, *Christ versus Religion*, p. 152.

[157]Acts 5:38-39, Phillips.

[158]*The Stream*, 15, No. 1 (February 1977), p. 13.

[159]Lee, *The Practical Expression of the Church*, p. 133.

[160]Lee, *Christ and the Church Revealed*, p. 198; *The Vision of God's Building*, pp. 69-70.

[161]Lee, *Christ versus Religion*, p. 115; *How to Meet*, pp. 27-30, 39, 66-67.

[162]Lee, *The Vision of God's Building*, p. 30.

[163]Lee, *Christ versus Religion*, p. 153.

[164]Ibid., p. 174.

[165]Lee, *The Practical Expression of the Church*, p. 138.

[166]Lee, *Christ versus Religion*, p. 34.

[167]Lee, *The Kingdom and the Church* (1971), p. 25.

[168]Lee, *Christ and the Church Revealed*, pp. 178, 227-30.

[169]Ibid., p. 144.

[170]Lee, *The Practical Expression of the Church*, p. 186.

[171]Lee, *God's Purpose For the Church*, p. 8.

[172]Lee, *Christ versus Religion*, p. 179.

[173]See note 124, above.

[174]Lee, *The Vision of God's Building*, p. 189.

[175]Lee, *The Economy of God*, p. 115.

[176]*The Stream*, 14, No. 3 (August 1976), p. 27.

[177]Lee, *The Vision of God's Building*, p. 172.

[178]Lee, *The Knowledge of Life*, p. 112.

4. An Evaluation of Witness Lee's Writings

[1]"The outstanding feature of Christianity today is teaching. Henceforth we must downgrade teaching and give first place over in our meetings to praising the Lord." Lee, *Christ and the Church Revealed*, p. 68.

[2]*The Stream*, 14, No. 4 (November 1976), p. 12; this theme is also prevalent at Local Church testimonial meetings.

[3]Lee, *How to Meet*, p. 243.

[4]Ibid., p. 253.

[5]Lee, *Concerning the Triune God–the Father, the Son, and the Spirit*, p. 11.

[6]Ibid., pp. 8-9.

[7]Jn. 14—16.

[8]See F. W. Grosheide, *Commentary on the First Epistle to the Corinthians*, New International Commentary on the New Testament (Grand Rapids: Eerdmans, 1953), pp. 386-87; see also Archibald Robertson and Alfred Plummer, *A Critical and Exegetical Commentary on the First Epistle of St. Paul to the Corinthians*, 2nd ed., International Critical Commentary (Edinburgh: T. & T. Clark, 1914), p. 373.

[9]John Peter Lange, *Commentary on the Holy Scriptures*, trans. Philip Schaff (New York: Charles Scribner's Sons, 1901), Vol. VI of the New Testament, *The Second Epistle of Paul to the Corinthians*, p. 58; Freeman, *Testimony of Church History*, p. 11.

[10]Cf. Lewis B. Smedes, *All Things Made New: A Theology of Man's Union with Christ* (Grand Rapids: Eerdmans, 1970), pp. 54-59.

[11]A Local Church in-house circular, "Revelations Received of the Lord Within the Period of 1920 to 1973," lists 46 such experiences of Lee's related to personal salvation and church emphases, and 22 related to church growth.

[12]E.g., Ps. 63:8; 84:2; 73:21; Prov. 23:15-17.

[13]Gen. 2:7 KJV; Lev. 17:11.

[14]Lev. 26:11, 30.

[15]Lk. 1:46 RSV.

[16]Mk. 12:30.

[17]Is. 1:18; Job 38:3 RSV; 40:7; Gen. 2:19-20; Rom. 12:1-2.

[18]John R. W. Stott, *Your Mind Matters* (Downers Grove: InterVarsity Press, 1972), p. 22. Cf. Col. 3:10; Eph. 4:23; 1 Cor. 2:15-16; 10:15.

[19]See Jude 8-9.

[20]Gen. 1:31, 3:17; Rom. 8:19-23.

[21]Jn. 3:16; Is. 65:17-22; 2 Pet. 3:10-13; Rev. 21—22.

[22]Lee, *The Economy of God,* p. 10.

[23]E.g., ibid., p. 106; *The Vision of God's Building,* pp. 171-72.

[24]Freeman, *Testimony of Church History,* pp. 5-6.

[25]Ibid., pp. 14-21.

[26]Lee, *Christ and the Church Revealed,* p. 40.

[27]John Murray, *Redemption Accomplished and Applied* (Grand Rapids: Eerdmans, 1955), pp. 146-47.

[28]Lee, *The Knowledge of Life,* p. 153.

[29]Lee, *The Experience of Life,* p. 159.

[30]Mickelsen, *Interpreting the Bible,* pp. 262-63.

[31]Testimony at a Local Church meeting focused on the type/antitype principle, citing the Old and New Testaments, the two Adams, the temple and the church, the apostolic church of Acts and the Local Church today. In each case, the first was a type and the second its fulfillment. As to the principle of "first biblical mention," Freeman uses Lev. 2:4 as the typological foundation of the doctrine of mingling (*Testimony of Church History,* p. 7).

[32]*The Stream,* 15, No. 1 (February 1977), p. 15.

[33]Gen. 1:26-28; 2:8-9.

[34]Lee, *The Four Major Steps of Christ,* p. 26.

[35]Ibid., pp. 19-20.

[36]Lee, *How to Meet,* p. 78.

5. The Local Church in Action

[1]John Lofland and Rodney Stark, "Becoming a World-Saver: A Theory of Conversion to a Deviant Perspective," *American Sociological Review,* 30, No. 6 (1965), pp. 862-75.

[2]William Bainbridge, *Satan's Power* (Berkeley: University of California Press, 1978), p. 12

[3]Lofland and Stark, pp. 862-75.
[4]Rosabeth Moss Kanter, *Commitment and Community* (Cambridge: Harvard University Press, 1972), pp. 165-91.
[5]Lofland and Stark, pp. 862-75.
[6]Ibid.
[7]Ibid.
[8]Spiritual Counterfeits Project letters and interview.
[9]Spiritual Counterfeits Project letters and interviews.
[10]Anthony Campolo, *Scientific Approach to the Study of American Cults* (Berkeley: 1978). This is a transcription of a lecture delivered in Los Angeles, 27 May 1978.
[11]Spiritual Counterfeits Project letters and interviews.
[12]Ibid.
[13]Kanter, pp. 165-91.
[14]Richard Delgado, "Religious Totalism: Gentle and Ungentle Persuasion under the First Amendment," *Southern California Law Review,* 51 (November 1977), p. 55.
[15]Spiritual Counterfeits Project interviews with ex-members.
[16]Lee, *Christ and the Church Revealed,* p. 129.
[17]Spiritual Counterfeits Project interviews with ex-members.
[18]Ibid.
[19]Lee, *The All-Inclusive Christ,* p. 190.
[20]Ibid., p. 157.
[21]Margaret T. Singer, "Coming Out of the Cults," *Psychology Today* (January 1979), p. 75.
[22]Campolo.
[23]Spiritual Counterfeits Project interviews with ex-members.
[24]Ibid.
[25]Angus I. Kinnear, *Against the Tide: The Story of Watchman Nee* (Eastbourne, England: Victory Press, 1973), pp. 131-32.
[26]Ibid., pp. 132-33.
[27]Spiritual Counterfeits Project interviews with ex-members.
[28]Ibid.
[29]Ibid.
[30]Singer, pp. 72-82.
[31]Ibid., p. 75.
[32]Ibid.
[33]Ibid., p. 80.
[34]Ibid., p. 75.
[35]Ibid., p. 79.
[36]Ibid., p. 75.
[37]Spiritual Counterfeits Project interviews with ex-members.
[38]Singer, p. 82.
[39]Ibid., pp. 80, 82.
[40]Ibid., p. 80.

[41]Eph. 2:14-20 NIV.

Appendix 1

[1]See Johannes Lindblom, *Prophecy in Ancient Israel* (Philadelphia: Fortress Press, 1962), pp. 299-311.

[2]David Haddon, "Thou Shalt Not Think," HIS magazine, December 1973, p. 10.

[3]Claudio Naranjo and Robert E. Ornstein, *On the Psychology of Meditation* (New York: Viking Press, 1971), pp. 163-67.

[4]Haddon, p. 12. Italics added.

[5]Sparks, p. 226.

[6]Faye Levine, *The Strange World of the Hare Krishnas* (Greenwich: Fawcett, 1974), p. 60.

[7]Mk. 12:30.

[8]Mt. 13:23, 15:16, 16:9, 24:15; Lk. 24:45; Jn. 8:43.

[9]Mt. 15:10; Mk. 7:14.

[10]Rom. 15:20-21.

[11]*The Stream,* 8, No. 1 (1 February 1970), p. 6.

[12]See *Occult Philosophy and Mystical Experience,* Spiritual Counterfeits Project Publication No. 0-6.

[13]In *Being Human: The Nature of the Spiritual Experience,* Ranald Macaulay and Jerram Barrs provide an excellent description of Platonic influences on Christian thinking. They cite Watchman Nee and Morton Kelsey as two examples of Bible expositors who have adopted the Platonic sacred/secular split.

[14]D. A. Rees, "Platonism and the Platonic Tradition," *The Encyclopedia of Philosophy* (New York: Macmillan, 1967).

[15]Hans Jonas, "Gnosticism," *The Encyclopedia of Philosophy* (New York: Macmillan, 1967).

[16]Ibid.

[17]Robert M. Grant, *Gnosticism and Early Christianity* (New York: Harper & Row, Publishers, 1966), p. 7.

[18]Ibid., p. 9.

Appendix 2

[1]Herman Ridderbos, *Paul: An Outline of His Theology* (Grand Rapids: Eerdmans, 1975), pp. 93-95.

[2]Ibid., pp. 120-21.